POETRY AND MIND

IDIOM INVENTING WRITING THEORY

Jacques Lezra and Paul North, series editors

POETRY AND MIND

TRACTATUS POETICO-PHILOSOPHICUS

LAURENT DUBREUIL

Fordham University Press *New York* *2018*

Visit us online at www.fordhampress.com.

Library of Congress Control Number: 2017960402

Printed in the United States of America

20 19 18   5 4 3 2 1

First edition

PREFACE

What one cannot compute, thereof one must speak. Computation is not limited to mathematical formalization; it also refers to the automaticity of neural activities, to what one came to name *cognition*. All "minds" *compute* in the sense that they all repeat relatively standard or stable procedures of thought, while tending to consistence. Quite notably, some types of minds function in a less stabilized manner than others, and, at any rate, no human agent "computes" the way an ordinary *computer* does. When we solve equations, process the visual stimuli that are turned into images within our brain, apply ourselves to the logical criteria of a regular philosophical demonstration, or do over and over again the exact "same" series of gestures, we are certainly drawn closer to the cognitive space. The next question is: Do we only think through computation? The interrogation is becoming all the more pressing as we consider language, literature, art, and creation (distinguished from trial and error or from mere invention). Moreover, we should not completely obliterate the fact that our rules, grammars, guidelines, or algorithms often fail—and that we sometimes, unexpectedly, find a way to move past their limits. The differences that are inherent in the *performance* of thought, bypassing "purely" repeatable operations, as well as the constitutive defects of organized procedures, all point at the possible existence of a noncognitive regime of thinking that I call *intellection*. If intellection stems from the differences and difficulties of cognition, the former should not be reduced or assimilated to the latter. We can think (through) the uncomputable. Poetry does it. Not because it would be connected with the antepredicative, nor be freer, but because it mobilizes multilayered cognition in order to displace it, to crack it open. The intellective work of poetry eminently shows that we can speak of what we cannot speak—and that such talk is worth more than the babbling of the ineffable. Our contemporary societies might well decide to favor the cognitive to such an extent that the intellective would simply be dismissed, discarded, or nullified. But, I say it plainly, a decision of this sort is akin to mind amputation and control. Systematically silencing the noncomputable range of thinking, then collectively abjuring the intellective ability to create, might turn us into more efficient computing machines (even though I would not even bet on this). Yet, we may wish to be more than maimed minds. Poetry is not only exemplary of the other contents and modes of thinking we can access; it decisively expands *noēsis*. In this book, I aim to demonstrate how cognitive processes are enrolled, altered, and extended by the intellective dimension of poetry.

Poetry and Mind is a case of, and for, *undisciplined* research, combining cognitive science with literary criticism, philology with "theory," and the "analytic tradition" with the broader conception of philosophy. The first theses here build upon the overall argument of my *Intellective Space*. In its approach to the literary, this book has affinities with some of my previous publications, most notably the articles "What Is Literature's Now?" and "On Experimental Criticism," as well as parts of my *Empire of Language* and two books so far only available in French, *De l'attrait à la possession* and *L'état critique de la littérature*. This being said, I did not introduce the qualification of poetry I am offering here before the 2015 *diacritics* article "On Poetry and Mind."[1]

This book also reacts to the current academic standardization of writing, in adopting—and modifying—the poetics of a discursive subgenre that is inspired by Ludwig Wittgenstein's *Tractatus Logico-Philosophicus*. The recourse to a method of exposition that aimed at anchoring thought in the most stringent constraints of linear rationality can only be judged in relation to the argument about the intellective excess *of* and *to* cognition. In other terms, a *tractatus poetico-philosophicus* neither eschews nor ridicules the ordering of epideictic thought: It proceeds from it but goes beyond.

Most numbered theses in Section 2 (that is, most of the volume) deal with poetry taken as a *collective* name. A series of "inserts" are added to these positions: They mainly address poetry on the *singulative* level, and many of them contain readings of specific works that are considered in the light of a given thesis. They do not exactly "illustrate" a more general idea, for they often bring novel elements to a discussion they concurrently modify. Other inserts are more technical or descriptive in nature. There is, then, a dual *inscription* or *insertion*: an insertion of detailed textual analyses within the argumentative, and "thetical," form and an inscription of a general problem within the singular reading of the poem. This overall disposition should allow readers to vary their own approach to the text: Each component could be read in isolation or as a stratum of one discourse. Any other interpretative montage is acceptable.

In its numbered paragraphs, the treatise displays a strong argumentative continuum. Still, the very sectioning of lemmas already introduces a sharp discontinuity that the further occurrences of inserts also strengthen. I believe in the heuristic powers of discontinuous continuity. It is troubling to see scholarly partisans of the fragmentary often compensating for the interruption of their own writing in maintaining a sort of undue historical thread (think of Giorgio Agamben, for instance). It is equally disturbing to notice that the dominant stylistics of knowledge seeks to conceal its inevitable discontinuity at all costs with cheap rhetorical devices or (now) "masses of data."

In the current climate of defunding the study of literature to the benefit of applied technical sciences, it may be more urgent than ever to establish that poetry both modifies and expands how, and what, we think. A war is being waged against the intellective extension of the mind and against the potentialities of noetic creation. This war is at once commercial, theoretical, and political; its ultimate goal is merely to erase thinking.[2] Neutrality on this matter is not a valid option. By becoming exclusively or even mainly "computational" (or bureaucratic), the humanities—as a field of inquiry—would lose any right to *be*. By believing in social engineering through the means of literature, rather than in the transformative potentialities of the latter, critical theory makes itself subservient to the "laws of the land" it should contest. By haphazardly importing technical tools from the quantitative sciences or half-understood "results" into humanistic research, one becomes ensnared in maladapted technicalities while ratifying the unidimensional. By putting the emphasis on prerequisite determinations, literary criticism and theory miss the raison d'être of their own objects while contributing willy-nilly to the goal of reducing mental capabilities and the livability of life.

What we need now, if we ever wish to renew the study of literary thinking, is to appropriate scientific descriptions without identifying them with procedures or tricks and without being *bounded* by them. We also need to abandon historicism, and any other similar empiricism or culturalism, without having to embrace an inane reduction to the "biological" or to "the given." We must construct corpora that are more, much more, than "global," and we should study many different languages, areas, and eras. Now, uncommensurability is such that we are certainly not about to renounce the arduous duties of the philological and the philosophical, without which comparisons just become readymade mechanisms that even up singularities. It finally goes without saying that no epistemic renewal of this magnitude will happen within the brackets of unimaginative prose and ideas. None of this means that we should relinquish the longstanding task of the literary disciplines. Quite the opposite: we just need to give away the pose and the buzz, the amateurish and the selfish, the vanities of technicism and the illusions of the code. And where could we find a more suitable example for this quest than in the very oeuvre of poetry?[3]

Poems are always quoted both in the original and in English translation; the two versions are connected with a bullet •. In most cases, I am the author of the translation; there are many exceptions, all duly noted. When the original is in a script other than Latin, I am only providing a transliterated version. Japanese or Chinese characters are additionally included.

In quotes, the sign | indicates the end of a line, whereas ¦ represents an internal pause (like a caesura), and the mark ⁝ identifies the end of a metrical unit within a line. The end of a stanza is symbolized with ¶. When the accentual content of a verse is considered, syllables in **bold** *receive a major stress, secondary stresses are underlined with small* dots, *and more minor stresses appear like* this. *If needed, synalœphas are also made typographically* obvious. *For syllabic length, I use the conventional signs of Western metrics: ⏑ for short, and – for long vocalic sounds. Regular* underlining *draws the reader's attention to the signifier. Digits with double square brackets refer the reader to the numbered inserts.*

POETRY AND MIND

0 What one cannot compute, thereof one must speak.

1 The mind happens to think, differently.

1.0 "The mind" is, at most, a conceptual index for *where* ideas, reflections, feelings, calculations, perceptions, or reasonings take place. It could also be understood as a *repertoire* for such operations, phenomena, or experiences. "The mind," then, refers to both a *set* and a *site*. It seems difficult to take the mental set and site to be completely independent from each other.

1.0.0 "The mind" certainly is a worn-out word. Its common usage still carries a false "body and mind" antinomy. Its translations across languages are inextricable, often literally haunted by *spirits* or *ghosts*. It has now been largely preempted by "analytic" philosophy and the scientific study of cognition. "Mind" is a term I will use nonetheless, sometimes trading the Latin etymon for the Greek root, thus speaking of the *noetic* as well as the *mental*, of *noēsis* rather than *mental activity*. This interplay of words, though not systematic here, should also *remind* us of the dual reference to the *set* and the *site*.

1.1 One thinks. One is thinking. Does one think because one is thinking? The *happening* of thinking is both action and virtual inscription.

1.1.0 *One* may be a human, an animal, a machine. And all humans are animals. And all animals may be machines, though this is much less obvious. At any rate, "the mind" is not—or not exclusively—the kind of computing machine we now know, or think, of.

1.1.1 *One* may be more than *one*. Even minimal mental operations already prepare the bifurcation we witness each time we consider our ways of thinking, or ourselves, or what "each time" could mean, and could refer to.

1.2 A mind is more than a brain. It includes an embodied neural system that should never be identified with one specific organ. Moreover, the brain itself is not exclusively nor primarily cortical: The "lower regions," the more inner and evolutionarily ancient parts, also give us emotions, balance, and memories. As for the role of the enteric nervous system, it appears to be more significant than once accepted. Then, minds are not wholly encapsulated in the bodies of individuals. They are routinely distributed through the emergence of group thinking, partially externalized to blocks of their environments (mnemonic objects and loci, papers and pens, books, laptops, and other prostheses), and potentially changed through exchange. The centripetal force of processes leading (back) to neural appropriation cannot conceal the concurrent and centrifugal impetus of the minds.

1.3 Thinking is not reduced to thought.

1.3.0 Let us use the word and category of *cognition* for mental operations that could be automated and produced according to common rules. While cognitive processes might fail, they seek equilibrium, thus tending to be *relatively* durable, consistent, and transparent. *Noise*—in the technical sense—is supposedly excluded, or negligible. Instituted, organized knowledge (and primarily "science") favors the cognitive regime of thought in the fabric of its own theories and practices.

1.3.1 *Intellection* is the differential and variable performance of thinking. Being created ad hoc, it is transient, and often singular, thus resisting automation. The cognitive defects of mental acts—when they lack stability, avoid standard consistence, arise through opacity, or become "blocked"—strengthen the advent, and imprint, of intellection.

1.3.2 The cognitive regime tries to enfold thought upon itself; the intellective attempts to unfold it through thinking.

1.3.3 The intellective stems from the *noise* of *noēsis.*

1.3.4 It is not—or not only—that thought is the remains of thinking. It is also that thought remains attached to the thinkable, whereas thinking does not need to.

1.3.5 The intellective space is where a mind might seek to go beyond the limitations of computability, of decidability.

1.3.6 If cognition emerges from the properties of the mind, intellection emerges from emergence and is doomed to be further transcribed at an *operational* level. But transcription is no equation.

1.4 The mind is multidimensional. It is not "wrong" to focus on just one dimension rather than adopting a broader view: It is "poor," deliberately simplifying, or congruent to specific (pedagogic, strategic, epistemic) goals.

1.4.0 A zero-dimensional mind is an ideal, immaterial point. At the extreme tip of methodic doubt, the Cartesian *res cogitans* • "the thing that is thinking" might have no body, no world, no god, and no place to be; it works as the very *intent* of thought. This contrasts with the "extended thing" • *res extensa*, that localizable body I may persuade myself to be living *in*. The punctual image of the mind may have never been other than some intended—transitional—fiction. The first cognitive paradigm of the 1970s essentially downplayed the material role of the "hardware" in the advent of thought.

1.4.1 More recent propositions suggest approaching the mind to the *extent* of its necessary embodiment.

1.4.2 The "*extended*-mind hypothesis" is bidimensional and addresses the ecological situation of intelligent agents, downloading parts of their noetic functions to a "peripheral" apparatus.

1.4.3 The intellective hints at a third axis, at *extension* beyond extendedness, through the eventful coelaboration of transient thinking.

1.4.4 The fourth dimension, time, deals with the gradual aspect of ideas (being assembled or constructed, appearing and sinking) and also with the noetic tenability of what is "the same time" to us. I say: noetic time is *tense* to us.

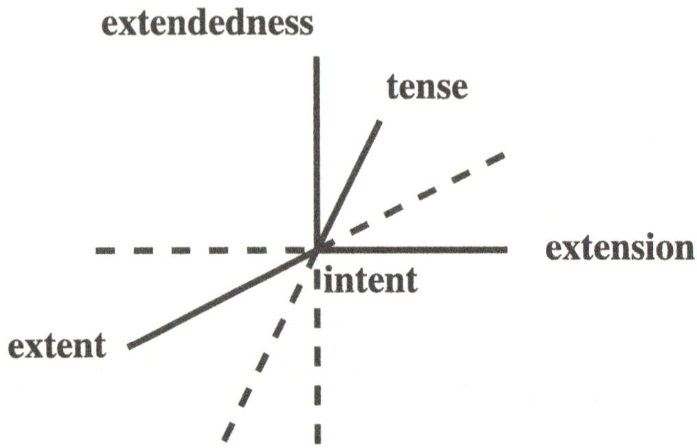

Figure 1. Dimensions of the mind: a diagrammatic representation

1.5 Human verbal language is a very powerful *organon* that makes us think differently.

1.5.0 Human verbal language guarantees cognitive routines through syntactic rules. It disseminates knowledge, it emphasizes logical sets, it enforces prescriptions. Words create zones of convergence and attractor basins for ideations that order our stream of thoughts. Attention disorders in humans accompany weakened verbal abilities; conversely, other "languaged apes" (like members of the *Pan* species) reach a new mental level that is not confined to incrementally added possibilities for expression. As a matter of fact, the bonobos who are endowed with human language do not speak much in general—but they think further.[1]

1.5.1 The paradox is this: Because human speech has to be granular, open-ended, flexible, and opaque enough to lend itself to possibly unlimited and unexpected usages, because it appears as a proliferating and quasi-autonomous entity, it is also the source for a lot of "noise" within communication. It operates and it also differentially performs. It "bootstraps" cognition while betraying the cognitive.

It introduces both more and less than we could say or think (or say we think, or think we say, or think we say we think, etc.).

1.5.1.0 The century or paradigm we are finally leaving was obsessed with this paradox. The novelty was the multidisciplinary obsession (certainly not the problem itself) as well as the energy deployed to comment upon or lament those difficulties, to deepen or erase them.

1.5.1.1 The practical success of information science—through its major recourse to binary logic and the legacy of founding figures like Alan Turing—constantly invites us to feel the inadequacy of "natural languages" (compared to the code), while promoting an ideal of computability that neglects the consequences of the halting problem or of constant Ω. Even from a mathematical viewpoint, the serial identifications of *noēsis* with thought, of thought with cognition, of cognition with algorithmic processes, should lead us to envisage the blind spots, defaults, and incapacities we have to cope with. Thus, computers, as such, do not prove we are Turing machines: They may have some inabilities that are also common to human minds but also more impressive reliability or consistence. But, so far, once they have to deal with the impossible or the unthinkable, they do not know what to do next. Or they select some probable scenario from a sort of prearranged list. Humans often do the same. But they can also bypass their limitations through speculation, intellection, creation.

1.5.2 Policing language or vaunting absolute free style will neither completely amend the cognitive pitfalls of speech nor liberate our spontaneous genius once and for all. It is through the iterable performance of cognition that intellection happens. The rules and disciplines of human language may be the unexpected paths leading to the intellective space.

1.6 Novel ideas arise through *trials and errors*, or through *invention and recombination*. And, one step further, they may be *created*, when one perceives the abyss and leaps. Creation will indeed need to be cognized, and somehow enfolded, which might even encompass automated or "bureaucratic" mental operations. However, what made the latter possible derives from a very dramatic move into an unexpected beyond, and back.

1.7 *Poiēsis* is a name I retain to speak of creative mental responses to the noncomputable, especially as they pertain to intellection *with* language.

1.8 *Poetry* is a verbal art that both extensively explores and shapes intensively the potentialities of *poiēsis*.

1.8.0 Poetry is thinking. It is not preverbal, prerational, prelogical. Percepts and emotions are there, though not as adversaries, or rivals, to the *res cogitans*.

1.8.1 Not all intellection is poetic.

1.8.2 The whole of poetry is not intellective, but the mental experience of poetic speech events relies on noetic *extension*. Poetry *changes our minds*.

1.8.2.0 If we intend to discuss what a poem allows us to fancy, feel, believe, or formulate, by simply "skipping" the prosodic aspects and directly branching ourselves with some "higher content" (be it conceptual, social-historical, moral, or "theoretical"), we may end up delivering *flat* or *one-sided* readings. Conversely, once it is acknowledged, the excess of and to cognition demands that we take great care in situating the regulations and calculations a text brings forward—and in describing how those rules are being done, undone, and abandoned. In this we may become capable of reclaiming for ourselves something of the conditions of creation we have just retraced.

1.8.2.1 A banal misconception is *technicism*. In his *Poetics*, Aristotle criticized those who describe poetry as the making of meters.[2] Almost two and a half millennia later, we unfortunately have to deal with the same unidimensional prejudice: The technique of the verse helps promote a cognitive reification of the poem—our sight is narrowed.

1.8.2.2 The intersection of cognitive science and literary studies holds promise, if and only if: we do not entrap the mental into the algorithmic (especially the deterministic), we recognize in *poiēsis* the possibility of disrupting the common order of thoughts, we accept to be touched in return by what we interpret.

1.8.2.3 The average, standard, historical, or ideal readers are ghosts that literary scholars live with. A typical reader's brain, as deciphered with fMRI or MEG machines, is just another specter. "Neurohumanists" who would condemn themselves to compare the scans of the readers' brain activity would not deal with anything more than the common, as long as they lack a theory for understanding differences and idiosyncrasies.

1.8.2.4 In the same vein, the "big data" of digital humanities plead in effect for the computational. Oddly enough, many defenders of those new tools do not perceive the connection between their own "mining" and the algorithmic rendition of cognition. Furthermore, "unpredictability, complexity, and abrupt shifts over time"[3] are notoriously hard to handle with vast amounts of information—and those three traits, precisely, are also strongly tied to poetic texts. This epistemic obstacle, once coupled with the discontinuity regarding the status of the algorithmic (from the "data" to "the brain"), logically expels, from research itself, the rich mental experience of reading poetry.

1.8.2.5 What happens to us with poems challenges what we believe we know about cognition. It eloquently shows there are more than rules and operations in thinking but also that such excess can only derive—and derail—from routines, patterns, and automation.

1.9 The literary performance of the form is informed by its mental *transform.*

2 The noetic experience of poetry both reveals and confirms the potential extension of the mind.

2.0 I *qualify* the noetic existence of poetry. I am not *defining* it. I am not installing an *in/out* gate. I am not even giving a series of traits that should be *reserved* to the poetic. Specificity is built through

Poetry . . .

(A1) is a noetic and discursive mode that is very widespread—and possibly universal—among human societies;
(A2) is both internally and externally contrasted with other—ordinary—modes of thought and speech-acts;
(A3) is enacted ad hoc, through discrete textual objects;

(B1) is differentially performed, with varying degrees of competence;
(B2) maximizes and dynamizes semantics;
(B3) is a linguistic construct that also operates in more than language(s);
(B4) uses imagery, especially in deploying the rhetorical armature of speech;

(C1) is a priori regulated through iterative systems;
(C2) is a priori regulated through linguistic re-organization;

(D1) tends to exceed its own algorithms;
(D2) is complex and highly incompressible;
(D3) incorporates cognitive dissonance and draws on non-consistent logical reasoning;
(D4) is aptly recursive and reflexive;

(E1) creates detachable, movable, and livable significations for psychological selves,
(E2) suggests "thinking experiments" for the unthinkable.

Figure 2. The mental experience of poetry: a research project

the singular assemblage of nonunique features. It does no more require a fixed number of features (all of them, most of them, . . .) to crystallize. Uniqueness is gauche conceptual framing.

2.1 *Poetry is a noetic and discursive mode that is very widespread—and possibly universal—among human societies.*

2.1.0 Let us consider poetry as *discourse* and not as the inherent quality of things that some texts would channel. As for the fact of language, it is as much before as in us. A poem is a *cosa mentale.*

2.1.1 Cultural relativism will not do; neither will historicism. The local configuration of entities cannot preclude by principle the promise of the universal. True, *poetry* is not *Dichtung*, *Dichtung* is not *shi*, and *shi* not *ci.* But who would believe that *poetry* in Milton and *poetry* in D. H. Lawrence have the exact same meaning? Or that chronologically contemporary authors such as Alfred de Musset and Victor Hugo are in complete agreement over the definition of a poem? Here, we primarily encounter the banal—though still troubling—issue of signification. The words of poetry allow us to suggest some meaning that will irreducibly be flexible and revisable.

2.1.2 It seems that in most—if not all—of the human societies we have a linguistic record of, something like poetry is to be found. Whereas this characterization is proleptic (the "something like" corresponds to the qualification we are beginning to detail), it does not entail that widely divergent practices were standardized in advance, under one label, for the argument's sake. The plurality of poetry—realized in songs, dances, psalmodies, in thousands of lines or in brief forms, acoustically or visually—is a mark of its differential *performalism.* We shall do justice to the extremely widespread and longstanding existence of poetic modes in human lives if we, as scholars, are able to reflect on a scale that would be more than global. Predetermined conceptual unification is inadequate; comparison is not enough. Innovative inquiries on pervasive literary categories will come from both broad and sound examination of a multitude of different traditions and languages in time and space.

2.1.3 The human mind is not a "blank slate"; it is not unbounded by biological constraints. Nor is it the sole output of a genetic software. It heavily depends on individual development, on the features of the anthropic worlds it evolves into, on the noetic prostheses it can rely upon. Like in other animal species, our capabilities outact our capacities. In the historical timeline, heritable changes in the biological makeup of the central nervous system are either genetic and quite slow (compared to our own lifespan) or epigenetic and less robust. Thus, the mind is configured by widely different conditions of existence. "Nature" in us encompasses the given as well as the physical determinations of evolving beings, which ultimately govern "growth," plasticity, and expression. There are limits to what we can do, achieve, and become. But the *phusis* of "culture" shows that ordered and meaningful symbolic networks outstretch seemingly "natural" capacities. Hence, arguing in favor of poetry as a biological adaptation really falls short. The omnipresence of poetry among humans is less a "fact of nature" than a second-order consequence of the physical commonalities between our worlds, endowments, and tools. Furthermore, the experience of poetry, in its own turn, alters our minds—or contributes to shift the moving barriers of our noetic capabilities.

2.2 *Poetry is both internally and externally contrasted with other—ordinary—modes of thought and speech-acts.*

2.2.0 A poem is extra-ordinary and is revealed as such. Even "found poetry" made of duplicated fragments of heterogeneous texts (advertising prospectuses or archival documents) stands in contrast with ordinary delivery, through selection, cut, or at least montage; it is an extreme case of *literature's response*.[1] Most often, poetic oeuvres get recited or typographically presented in a particular manner. The Kuna indigenous people have developed a stratified verbal art, with diverse manners of speaking (each having different morphological, syntactical, lexical properties). Only some of them are used in poetry, which readily signifies that a piece will not belong to more banal communication. In other contexts, and without music or heavily ritualized delivery, nongrammatical pauses indicate a dissimilarity with usual discourse. For better or worse, the North American cliché of ecstatic or tearful recitation in poetry reading festivals as well as the conventional phrasing of many slammers are oral signs of the unusual regime of poetry. The discontinuous *insertion* of poems in other modes of speech participates in this textual "revelation." [[1]]

1. *Poetic inscriptions in prose.*

In what might unfortunately be one of the last documented pieces of the Austronesian oral literature in Araki, the tale of the rat and the octopus (as told by Lele Moli) is suddenly interrupted by this brief song:

Tata ha mae ¦ ha vitia hinia
ha re lici horo lag ¦ horo lag
tam re mae ¦ tam re mae
•
Dad shall come ¦ I shall tell him
let the wind blow ¦ the wind blow
and when you go back ¦ when you go . . .[1]

This happens just twice over the course of the tale. In addition to the shift introduced by the singing voice (instead of the delivery of the storyteller), elements of repetition and parallelism, as well as metalinguistic markers (the song is attributed to the birds, with the sentences "and they began to sing like this" • "mo vavere sohe nene mo de," "and they went on like this . . . the birds starting to sing again" • "mo v̈a, va m̃aci mo le vavere mo de"[2]), announce and emphasize the poetic. Moreover, the lyrics are not in Araki but are either an import from another language or a well-crafted linguistic mixture. The poem is especially extraneous.

There is not always a clear agreement on what is an "inset poem" in the Torah,[3] although common characteristics facilitate identification, such as the use of a word like *shîr*—to sing—before the quote of a character given in direct speech (a configuration comparable to the Araki example), as well as the recourse to *parallelismus membrorum* within the hymns, laments, curses, or prayers themselves. Doubts or ambiguities on the status of some fragments may still remain, but the perception of internal discursive inflexions cannot be revoked in doubt.

In *prosimetrum* as a genre, be it relying on straightforward signs or not, boundaries are often sharp, for the purpose is precisely to grant a higher evocative power to poetry by embedding it into nonpoetry. Still, concurrently, a sort of marginal assimilation could occur, as if the poetic were contaminating unmarked discourse. Sima Xiangru's "*Fu* on the Imperial park" •上林賦 is all about "boundaries" • 疆 (*jiāng*) and "borders" • 界 (*jiè*), intended to "curb excess" • 禁淫 (*jìn yín*), as its first sentences indicate.[4] The moralizing perspective is a paradoxical pretext to a rich, overwhelming, and effusive description of the park. While modern editions demarcate the two regimes of speech used in this *fu*, the prosaic parts are touched by the exuberant wording of the depiction, as when the observer of the park is said—in "nonpoetry"—to be "dizzy and dazed, confounded and confused" • 縝紛軋芴, 芒芒怳忽 (*zhěn fēn zhá wù, máng máng huǎng hū*),[5] a phrase in which sound repetitions abound (especially in this possible reconstruction of the Old Chinese phonetic: *t̑i̯ĕn p'i̯wən ·ăt mii̯wət mwâng mwâng xwâng xmwət*).[6] In Dante's *Vita nuova*, all the quoted poems are unequivocally introduced and commented upon, the emphasis being on textual *divisions*. Now, metrical elements surreptitiously infiltrate the philological, as when assonant hendecasyllables watermark the factual explanation of a sonnet, thus connecting the quote of the poem with a poeticized commentary, as in "e dico che͡ io ¦ hoe ciò per**du**to. | La seconda parte ¦ comincia **qui**vi: | 'Amor, non già.'" • "and I tell that which I have lost. The second part begins thus: 'Love, it is not.'"[7]

---

1. Alexandre François, *Araki: A Disappearing Language of the Vanuatu* (Canberra: Pacific Linguistics Research School of Pacific and Asian Studies, 2002), 214–215. Here and below, I am using François's translation.

2. Ibid.

3. James W. Watts, "'This Song:' Conspicuous Poems in Hebrew Prose," in *Verse in Ancient Near Eastern Prose*, ed. Johannes De Moor and Wilfred Watson (Neukirchen: Neukirchener Verlag, 1993), 345–358. See also James W. Watts, *Psalms and Story: Inset Hymns in Hebrew Narrative* (Sheffield: Sheffield Academic Press, 1992).

4. Zong-Qi Cai, ed., *How to Read Chinese Poetry: A Guided Anthology* (New York: Columbia University Press, 2008), 61; English translation by David Knechtges.

5. Ibid., 64.

6. I am using the reconstructions given by Tor Ulving, *Dictionary of Old and Middle Chinese* (Gothenburg: Acta Universitatis Gothoborgensis, 1997). Thanks to Junting Huang for his help on this point.

7. Dante, *Vita nuova*, VII; my translation from the Italian.

2.2.1 In writing, lineation is an obviously prevalent sign—though it is neither universal nor sufficient. Many cuneiform tablets already divide poems in the same way "we" do. A new breaking up of lines could always turn a newspaper article into (admittedly, mediocre) free verse. In addition, some scripts tend to be reserved to poetry writing, like *nasta'līq* in Arabic. Aldus Manutius, who apparently invented italics in print, claimed that the model for his font was Petrarch's own writing in the holograph manuscript of the *Canzoniere*—and, for several decades in the sixteenth century, verses came to be almost systematically italicized in editions printed in many cultural centers of the Renaissance: Venice, Florence, Paris, or Lyons. All this is convention and artifice until some sense is made out of it. It remains that the frequent recourse to strong markers of differences—all the more so, if they are readily identifiable—advertises the singular modes of poetry and "primes" us.

2.3 *Poetry is enacted ad hoc, through discrete textual objects.*

2.3.0 Like literature, poetry is both singulative and collective. Each work is able to modify our previous understanding of poetry. Singulative variation is the dual product of writing and interpretation. Without the supplementary and collective possibility of recognizing poetry, we would isolate self-defining speech events. Qualifying shared traits without conducting closer readings is, by function, a partial endeavor and is intended to be complementarily displaced by ad hoc propositions. Some convergence between the singulative and the collective viewpoints is to be expected. Necessary discrepancies will remain.

2.3.1 In 1823, Goethe told Eckermann "all my poems are occasional poems" • "alle meine Gedichte sind Gelegenheitsgedichte."[2] The overall discussion was about the links between reality and creation. Goethe advocated a recourse to "the world" and admonished authors to study and belabor each time "a special case."[3] I'd like to distort the sentence somehow and see in the *occasion*—the circumstance or *kairos*—the very mark of a poem. *A poem* is tied to its circumstance; it emerges from it. *Poetry* serves as a preexisting collective body whose contours are modified by each textual occasion.

2.3.2 A great poem *promises* the universal. We should not wish to restrict it to the specifics of its composition or to identify it with one current reading. We should avoid at all cost to turn it into a fable about "the nature of the human mind." [[2]]

2.4 *Poetry is differentially performed, with varying degrees of competence.*

2.4.0 "Performance" is deliberately broad, and it covers uses of the voice, prosody, gestures, rhythms, signs, words, cognition. Diachronic and synchronic divergences in delivery shape the noetic existence of each poem.

2. *Thinking the universal and the singular at the beginning of Homer's* Odyssey.

> Ándra moi énnepe, moûsa, polútropon, hòs mála pollà
> plágkhthē, epeì Troíēs hieròn ptolíethron épersen
> •
> Speak through me, Muse, of a man, canny, enduring, who
> wandered a lot, after he sacked the sacred citadel of Troy.[1]

The opening lines of *The Odyssey* speak of *a* man ("ándra"), a man whose characteristics and deeds are summarized before becoming the very matter of the epic. The initial *captatio benevolentiæ* resides in dazzling alliteration—the first mentioned epithet of Odysseus ("polútropon," both *canny* and *enduring*) is immediately echoed in "pollà | plágkhthē, epeì Troíēs . . . ptolíethron" and in delaying the formal identification of the main character—the hero is only named on line 21, or roughly after two minutes of recitation, in a sort of cantillating modulation: "antithéō Oduseî" • "godlike Odysseus."[2] The verbal artwork manifests itself: We need to listen carefully to the speech of the goddess. A shared noetic space is opened, one whose polarities are the *I* of the speaker ("me" is the second word of *The Odyssey*), the *Muse* who is putting the epic words ("énnepe"—lit. "speaking from within"—being etymologically tied to *epos*) in the mouth of the poet—and in *us*. For *we* appear in the poem, on line 10: "speak to us too" • "eipè kaì hēmîn." "Homer" is speaking to us; he is also spoken by the Muse, and, with us, he is listening to the story he is telling. This prologue describes a mental operation that comments on both the tradition and practice of composition. The legend has been said more than once; we now want it to be told to "us too." Scripts are known and retrieved by the poet's brain, which is why the goddess (as well as the inspired and remembering mind) is invited to begin the tale "from whatever point" • "tôn hamóthen ge."[3] The first two minutes of the canto have given us an explanation of the chain of interlocution we partake in, a compact summary of the plot (the difficult return of Odysseus from Troy to Ithaca), and a demonstration of the qualities we need in order to savor the art of the poem. Beside all the general lessons one could draw from the singular adventure of one man, beside the narrative tradition and rules of oral composition, beside our noetic commonalities and what they allow in terms of understanding and participation, the introduction of *The Odyssey* is showing how the poetic is being redefined anew, here and now.

---

1. Homer, *Odyssey*, canto I, lines 1–2; here and below, my translation from the Greek.
2. Ibid., canto I, line 21.
3. Ibid., canto I, line 10. On the issue of cognitive scripts in Homer, also see Elizabeth Minchin, *Homer and the Resources of Memory: Some Applications of Cognitive Theory to the Iliad and the Odyssey* (Oxford: Oxford University Press, 2001).

2.4.0.0 At a minimum, a silent reading is *performing*—not only "processing"—a poem. A text could be more obviously and collectively embodied when it supports singing, dancing, public recitation, or theatrical representation. On all continents, folk poetry, if tuned to music, tends to have a choral element. Antiphonary structures are ubiquitous, and listeners are invited (often required) to join in. Poems undoubtedly acquire vital meaning through the fact of being not only repeated but also sung in unison. Such mind coupling, with individuals being synchronized in a group, allows for both cohesion and subjective attachment. The specifics of each performance are able to channel, enhance, and alter the appreciation or interpretation of a text. [[3]]

3. *Meanings of oral performance in sung and recited poetry.*

The dialogue between groups of singers (or a soloist and a choir) is necessary in the most diverse settings, from the praise poem of the Podzos in Mozambique to the questions-and-answers of the Malagasy *hainteny*, from the alternating couplets of the *cautal* of the Fiji Islands to the contemporary rock concert, where enraptured fans add to the polyphony of the refrains. Highly skilled modes of poetic delivery are less "democratic," but they similarly mold the understanding and pleasure of their audience. The Âşik minstrels of Turkey practice the genre of *leb-değmez*: With a needle between their lips, they utter lipograms avoiding the consonants *b*, *p*, *m*, *v*, and *f*. There, the virtuosity of textual composition is highlighted and prolonged by recitation. The Malayo-Polynesian *roro* repeats the same short couplet, "initially slowly, but usually hurriedly with a rising inflection,"[1] so the pleasure of the song derives from its reiteration and deformation through time. The artful coincidence or deliberate disconnect between melody and words also affects the mental construction of a piece. When, at the end of the first scene in the first act of John Adams's opera *Nixon in China*, Richard Nixon is stammering "News has a kind of mystery," singing "news" twelve times in a row, then "has a has a has a has a kind of mystery has a has a has a kind of mystery," with the final *y* of "mystery" stretching over eleven notes, the grotesque dimension of the character is made even more unmistakable than by reading Alice Goodman's brilliant libretto.

1. Jack A. Tobin, *Stories from the Marshall Islands* (Honolulu, University of Hawai'i Press, 2002), 8.

2.4.0.1 It also happens that the melody or the voice accompanying a poem ends up overwhelming the words themselves. Despite Richard Wagner's desire to design a *Gesamtkunstwerk*, when listening to the end of *Tristan*'s first act, one may be more moved by the voices and melody than by the dialogue ("Tristan! Isolde!"). Conversely, the interest in performance or in sociological and anthropological contexts should not become an excuse for ruling out in advance the literary qualities of songs and recitations.

2.4.0.2 Oral performance may be ritualized, thus becoming an efficacious system of conventions that will underscore discrete textual events. [[4]]

2.4.0.3 Oral performance is much less peripheral to poetry than it is to other literary discourses. Even in an age dominated by solitary and silent readings, we feel the urge to *voice* the text. There is an oral and aural inscription in each poem, whose sonic, rhythmic, and melodic envelopes are more evidently perceived through a voiced performance. Such inscription is the very dynamics of contemporary experiments in "sound poetry," from Christian Bök to Cosima Weiter.

2.4.0.4 *Writing* poetry (copying, printing it) is another performance. [[5]]

2.4.1 Instead of seeing the differential as a halo, we can, here too, speak of capabilities. What the poem says is not what most readers (even with comparable backgrounds) agree it says: It is also everything that could be expressed about it. I am myself a mutable interpreter whose discourse is conditioned by the extension of the piece I am analyzing.

2.4.2 There are gradients of competence in all aspects of poetic performance. Some texts require a high level of practice.

2.4.2.0 If we leave aside the high form of lyrical singing or the extraordinary demands of improvised composition, the "simple" task of reading aloud a poem requires skill and practice, as soon as one wishes to go beyond the stage of childish recitation. Some oeuvres are also more demanding than others. There, the inscription of performance is *training* the reader. [[6]]

2.4.2.1 Different manners of reading have vastly different neural signatures, as both subjective reports and recent fMRI experiments

4. *Ritualization of poetic performance.*

In traditional *al-taghroode*, the Bedouin chants of the Camel Tribes, long vowels are lengthened in an exaggerated manner. This is an invitation to play with vocalic length at key moments. The medieval Western troubadours and the Chinese authors of *ci* reemployed tunes for their lyrics. In those latter examples, the rules of public performance (and the need to adjust already known melodies to novel lines) predetermined the unfolding of the poem.

Various modes of delivery are occasionally combined. Both Chinese traditional theater and Australian "sand stories" use at least three ways of voicing the text: singing, speaking, and reciting (in Chinese); singing, talking, and humming (in Australian Aranda).[1] Not all modes are conducive of poetry. In ancient Greek theater (where plays were only in verse), we find a triadic model as well. Singing and speaking were the two opposite poles. In moments of transition between the sung and the spoken, or in intentional shifts, a third mode was certainly used, maybe close to *Sprechgesang* or to the Chinese recitation based on a strategic use of percussions. Outside of the profuse variability of versification in songs, Greek tragedies sometimes mobilized two different models of lines—the long catalectic trochaic tetrameter and the shorter, supposedly "conversational," iambic trimeter. Those two directions may have commanded inflections in the voice and style of the actor as well. At the level of an individual oeuvre, a writer like Allen Ginsberg explored diverse ways of embodying his texts. He would select a kind of modulated diction sustained by musical *beats*, jazzing his lyrics and thereby stressing the importance of African American arts in the constitution of his poetry; he would declaim, or simply *howl*, like he did in the early recorded reading of . . . "Howl."

Onstage performance of voice, gesture, "body language," and gait is also able to support, expand, and alter poetic texts. Masks with fixed facial expressions are used as sound amplification and as visual reminders of the sentiment or behavior of the character. In ancient Indian drama (often a mixture of Sanskrit and Prakrit and of verse and prose), the slightest aspects of textual embodiment were conventionalized early on, in treatises such as Bharata Muni's *Nātyaśāstra*, defining everything up to the position of the fingers of the left hand or the tiniest vocal inflexions.

---

1. On Australian "sand stories," see Jennifer Green, *Drawn from the Ground* (New York: Cambridge University Press, 2014).

5. *Some aspects of poetic calligraphy.*

Jewish micrography, while not restricted to poetry, often used psalms to create with letters an image that would be appropriate to the topic, for example, a hunt scene with a dog gripping a hare's foot in its mouth commenting on the biblical lament of the people of Israel once abandoned by God to its enemy.[1] In Islamic and specifically Ottoman arts, images were formed with excerpts of the Qur'an, like the eighteenth-century calligraphy in the form of a ship at sea, now in the collections of the New York City Metropolitan Museum of Art. In East Asia, the consubstantial link between poetry and epigraphic or calligraphic presentation is unmistakable. The high craft of medieval illumination exerted a durable influence on the ensuing conception of poetry, as evidenced by Arthur Rimbaud's *Illuminations* or Abdelkebir Khatibi's notion of *intersigne*. The more modest and private practice of copying verses for one's own in notebooks or diaries—a habit that was largely encouraged in the romantic and Victorian eras—or even the use of special, and often kitsch, fonts to enhance the presentation of verses on blogs and homepages partakes in the everyday performance of poetry. Finally, amimetic typography is, in itself, a necessary dimension of poetic experiments like Stéphane Mallarmé's *Un coup de dés*, Frankétienne's *L'oiseau schizophone*, or the *words in liberty* • *parole in libertà* of Italian futurism.

1. This example is mentioned in Dalia Rith-Halperin, *Illuminating in Micrography: The Catalan Micrography Maḥzor—MS Heb 8°6527 in the National Library of Israel* (Leiden: Brill, 2013), 204, pl. IV.

attest.[4] Denying those dissimilarities is illusory and is often a symptom of reactionary anti-intellectualism. "Close reading" is a technique with a particular history, but the phrase could also be used as a generic category to refer to any skilled and careful noetic performance one may become able to produce by studying and interpreting literary texts.

2.5 *Poetry maximizes and dynamizes semantics.*

2.5.0 Once we have been primed by the poetic *dispositif*, we conventionally enter a *maximal semantic world*. The slightest element could now make sense to us, in interrelation with the rest of the poem and other parts of the corpus we select. Meaninglessness is always of the second degree: It is not a semantic lack, it is not "without any sense," it is the intense subtraction of the maximal potentiality to *mean*.

6. *Synalœphas and Petrarch's poetic aims.*

Petrarch uses many synalœphas in the creation of his verses. A synalœpha consists in amalgamating two vocalic sounds in order to count one syllable (instead of two), often by turning a vowel into a semivowel. It is quite deceptive and virtuosic. In practice, even very experienced reciters like Roberto Benigni tend to replace at least some synalœphas with elisions, which are easier to perform. But the study of Petrarch's manuscripts leaves no doubt: He used both synalœphas and elisions, and we have no reason to consider that he randomly selected one over the other. In fact, given the abounding synalœphas, reading aloud—in Italian—the poems of the *Canzoniere* demands uncommon verbal agility. This is in line with the overall Petrarchan poetics combining the sophistication of its artifacts with an attention to sound. One could almost doubt it possible ever to utter in eleven syllables:

fior, frondi, herbe, ombre, antri, onde, aure soavi

•

flowers, fronds, herbs, shades, caves, waves, smooth breezes.[1]

And the whole impossibility of poetic speech once confronted with death and absolute love is suddenly heard in our own defective stutter.

---

1. Petrarch, *Canzoniere*, poem 303, line 5; my translation from the Italian. In 1525, Pietro Bembo already stressed the extreme particularity of this line in his *Prose della volgar lingua* (Bologna, Italy: CLUEB, 2001), 92–93 [par. II, xvii, 10].

2.5.0.0 In poems, even humble typographic marks are signifying. Some authors, for instance, are real artists of the dash. [[7]]

2.5.0.1 The possibility for phonemes or graphemes to reorganize themselves—and *mean*—is conventionally granted at the outset of a poem. The semantic force field of poetry allows us to witness the very process of semanticization, i.e., how we can endow any token with meaning. [[8]]

2.5.0.2 Regardless of their main objects, some *arts of readings* are chiefly poetic in nature or structure. [[9]]

2.5.0.3 Another representation of poetic semantics—of both its dynamics and boundaries—would concern extremely rare words and neologisms. [[10]]

7. *Notes for a poetics of the dash in Emily Dickinson and Gérard de Nerval.*

Both Nerval and Dickinson use the em-dash for opening parallel propositions and for disjointing elements, as would be expected. Nerval ends his "Delfica" with "—And nothing disturbed the severe portico" • "—Et rien n'a dérangé le sévère portique"[1] to stress the opposition between the immutable gate and the prophetic promise on the return of the ancient gods. Dickinson creates alternatives in writing "By Stretch of Limb—or stir of Lid—."[2] Both poets also use the dash to transcribe the very process of thinking. For instance, Dickinson's line "A long—long Sleep—A famous—Sleep"[3] is not "A long, long Sleep, a famous Sleep." The first version renders the performance of writing; the "emendated" verse is a more pedestrian epanorthosis. In the manuscript, the second capital *A* indicates a new beginning, as if we were reading a second, internal, *incipit* for the same poem. In Nerval's "I am the tenebrous,—the widower,—the unconsoled" • "Je suis le ténébreux,—le veuf,—l'inconsolé,"[4] the dash conveys a sense of implacable accumulation that the commas alone (added by the poet, even though they are not typographically required) would not create. Dickinson's text "Growth of Man—like Growth of Nature—" ends with "By no Countenance—,"[5] and this final dash becomes another sign of the infinite growth of *phusis*. Beyond writing conventions, punctuation is intensified and belongs to the idiosyncratic signification of a poem.

---

1. Gérard de Nerval, "Delfica," line 14 (in *Les chimères*); here and below, my translation from the French.
2. Emily Dickinson, *Complete Poems* (Boston: Little, Brown, 1960), 326 [poem 654].
3. Ibid.
4. Nerval, "El desdichado," line 1 (in *Les chimères*).
5. Dickinson, *Complete Poems*, 367–368 [poem 750].

2.5.0.4 Asemantic poetry does not exist. Glossolalia expresses the signification of meaninglessness. The "transrational" *zaum'* only makes the indeterminacy of meaning more palpable.

2.5.1 Maxima go with higher velocity. In the wake of Russian formalism, Jan Mukařovský rightly elaborated on dynamic semantics and their psychological nature.[5] Associations of words, changes of directions, happen more, and more frequently, in poems than in ordinary regimes of speech. Our minds may have to refocus several

8. *Attentional hyperesthesia and the role of the signifier in William Shakespeare's sonnet 119.*

What potions have I drunk of Siren tears
Distill'd from limbecks foul as hell within,
Applying fears to hopes and hopes to fears,
Still losing when I saw myself to win!
What wretched errors hath my heart committed
Whilst it hath thought itself so blessèd never!
How have mine eyes out of their spheres been fitted
In the distraction of this madding fever!
Oh, benefit of ill! now I find true
That better is by evil still made better,
And ruin'd love when it is built anew
Grows fairer than at first, more strong, far greater:
So I return rebuk'd to my content,
And gain by ills thrice more than I have spent.[1]

In Shakespeare's "What potions have I drunk . . . ," I can isolate the recurrence of two syllables throughout the sonnet: on one hand **il*, in *distill'd*, *still* (twice), *ill* (twice), *built*, and (in reverse) *limbeck*; on the other **fi*, in *fears* (twice), *spheres*, *fitted*, *fever*, *benefit*, and (graphically) *of ill*, *find*, *first*. "Ill" is the very name of love in the text, so the insistence of **il* works like an internal rhyme, bordering on obsession. "This madding fever" is a consequence of drinking "potions . . . of Siren tears . . . distill'd from limbecks." In parallel, the dissemination of **fi* looks like another *textual* distillation—or, to use Shakespeare's word, a "distraction," in the etymological sense—of "fever" and "fears," as if the signs of the poem were now performing the same kind of chemistry the *I* has been subjected to. If **il* readily corresponds to *ill*, the only word equivalence for **fi* would be the Greek letter *phi* (by trying to take into account its likely pronunciation during the great vowel shift). Now, φ (or a distorted version of the letter) was sometimes used as a symbol by alchemists for "distillate," so **fi* might appear to be the operator of the poem both on the thematic and rhematic planes.

A reading such as the one I have just offered is constrained by the historical and by the internal coherence of the text and corpus. Further procedures could attempt to check the Bard's direct knowledge of alchemy, to take **fi* as a *key* (this would be for *The Shakespeare Code* or *The Letter and the Siren*), to turn this distillation into an example of a quasi-metaphysical property of language or reality, and so on. I would rather state that, by keeping up with the pace of maximal poetic signification, I have found supplementary *positional meanings* for a priori asemantic tokens (*il, *fi). Those meanings are positional, for they are ad hoc (one cannot readily export them to other texts, even ones authored by Shakespeare) and coelaborated by the reader. They are not unbound, and we have here a good case of the interaction between the noetic (maximal semantics) and the social-historical (the institution of alchemy, the diachronic changes within one language). We might deal with the opposite of what psychologists call "inattentional blindness." While reading poetry, we may reach a kind of linguistically mediated "attentional hyperesthesia," where normally insignificant and imperceptible details get tracked down and then rendered meaningful.

1. William Shakespeare, *Sonnets*, poem 119. I am reproducing the spelling of the 1964 ed. published by the University of London Press.

9. *Poetic reading in Ferdinand de Saussure's paragrams and Jacques Derrida's dissemination.*

Saussure's *paragrams* and Derrida's *dissemination* of the signifier are elements of reading borrowed from the experience of poetry. For years Saussure sought in the lines of ancient epos and lyric the hidden names of divinities and heroes, before giving up his quest. He grew unconvinced of his own hypothesis: Despite the wealth of data he gathered, he had no proof that paragrams were a *system* of composition. In fact, embedded words and phonemes may be assembled by the author or even commented upon. (This is quite common in Greek tragedies, one of the most striking examples being Sophocles's Ajax, who analyzes his own name *Aias* as the repetition of the interjection *aí • alas.* I will later add other examples of the same kind.) But such operations do not have to form a rule. In *Glas*, Derrida sees in *gl* the gist of deconstruction in both Hegel's and Genet's texts. Here, and in many other instances, Derrida tends to source dissemination in language or in deconstruction itself. It seems more convincing to consider it a part of an art of reading. One of Derrida's moves was precisely to integrate "literary" modes of interpretation into the discussion of all possible texts and generally to treat all writing as belonging to a maximal semantic world.

times over the course of a poem (this is Michael Riffaterre's "retroactive reading"). Multistable meanings are being mobilized, and we oscillate between different strange attractors, never completely *finishing* the course. We do not exhaust the meaning of a poem; we are exhausted by it. [[11]]

10. *A screen-word at the end of Aimé Césaire's* Notebook of a Return to the Native Land.

"*Verrition,*" the final word of Aimé Césaire's *Notebook of a Return to the Native Land,* has been heavily discussed, and it is translated in English as, for instance, "revolvolution" or "veerition."[1] Long considered to have been coined by Césaire himself, *verrition* in French is rather a *hapax* that one finds in the lexicon of the nineteenth-century author and gastronome Brillat-Savarin to describe the circular movements of the tongue between teeth and gums and the lips. This sense is very adequate, since the last lines of the *Notebook* also evoke "the malefic tongue of the night" • "la langue maléfique de la nuit."[2] The final "immobile *verrition,*" as oxymoronic as it is, would thus refer to the now silent moves of the tongue at the end of a long poem. It remains that Césaire gave rather elusive explanations on this topic across the years and that he might have created the word on the sole basis of its Latin root.

When we encounter an unknown word, we adopt different and complementary strategies to decipher it. Analysis, etymology, and analogical or wild guesses are the most obvious paths. Independently of any understanding of **verri-*, the suffix *-tion* normally indicates a process, which already gives us a final contradiction (leading to the question: How could anything dynamic be "immobile?"). Latin *verro* is banally *to sweep, to clean* by brushing away. In poetry, it rather means *to drive away* or *to drag*, sometimes *to obliterate*. Within the dense intertextuality of Césaire's *Notebook* and given its oft elevated language, the poetic use of *verro* is to be favored. With less philological expertise, one could notice that *verrition* is literally close to *versification* or *verification* and that **ver*, in French, phonically evokes *verre* • *glass*, *vers* • *verse*, and *vers* • *toward*. The link with *verse* would not surprise, and *verrition* could even look like a truncated *versification*, naming the end of free verse in its final effacement. The directional meaning (*toward*) emphasizes the oxymoron. *Glass* would be a "self-reflection" on *verrition* as a *screen-word*, as a term that is both an obstacle to "word decoding" and a mirror to different sorts of semantic projection. In twentieth-century French Caribbean poetic writing (in Aimé Césaire, Saint-John Perse, and Édouard Glissant, in particular), an attraction toward the resourceful opacity of rare words is common[3] and situates a sort of inner, francophone, exoticism. Finally, wild guesses are another option, relying on sound symbolism, a long-debated problem that recently got revived through evidence of translinguistic decoding (including the "kiki-bouba" effect) and sound iconicity.

A wealth of psychology experiments in humans with or without language disabilities, in adults as well as children or teenagers, would tend to suggest that lexical comprehension uses one general pathway in the brain for words and "pseudowords." It is sometimes hypothesized that the encounter with new words elicits a search process at higher levels in the same way other terms do, but with less or no perspective of semantic consolidation. Césaire's text encourages us to accomplish such cognitive integrations, but the incompleteness of those operations points toward something more. Whatever the meanings we may attribute to *verrition*, the word precisely signifies in exhibiting both the cognitive underpinnings of semantic decoding and their inability ultimately to retain one "target." Veracious *verrition* is a series of unfinished algorithmic selection processes where each found equilibrium impinges on each constructed meaning.

---

1. *Revolvolution* appears in Aimé Césaire, *Notebook of a Return to my Native Land*, trans. Mireille Rosello and Annie Pritchard (Newcastle: Bloodaxe, 1995), 135; *veerition* in *Notebook of a Return to the Native Land*, trans. Clayton Eshleman and Annette Smith (Middleton, Conn.: Wesleyan University Press, 2001), 51. For an overview, see Carrie Noland, *Voices of Negritude in Modernist Print: Aesthetic, Subjectivity, Diaspora, and the Lyric Regime* (New York: Columbia University Press, 2015), 37–44.

2. Césaire, *Notebook of a Return to my Native Land*, 134 (for the French version); my translation from the French.

3. See Neal Allar, *Poetry of Relation*, PhD diss., Cornell University, 2016.

2.5.2 Were natural languages unambiguous, transparent, and perfect, then semantic extensibility and rapidity would have little appeal to us.

2.5.2.0 There is no "language of thought." And there is no universal map of word semantics "in the brain." Commonalities of experience pass for commonalities of meaning; logical categories are claimed to be words. This is why, in the most advanced experiments of brain "reading," very referential nouns—like *hand* or *cat*—are recognizable by their neural signature. Basic logical links—like *yes* and *no*—are also identifiable, with some accuracy. Verbs or less referential nouns, whose experience is much more diffuse, are extremely difficult to decipher with today's techniques: Even *to eat* or *to speak* are equivocal. Poetry is quite far ahead.

2.5.2.1 Do "language and literature reflect the nature of cognition"?[6] No. Through language, literature reflects on nature and cognition.

2.6 *Poetry is a linguistic construct that also operates in more than "language(s)."*

11. *Semantic bistability in Sophocles's* Antigone *(ll. 334–384).*

The choral ode devoted to mankind in Sophocles's *Antigone* is built on semantic oscillation. The first words of the *stasimon* are "pollà tà deiná" • "there are many fearful/dangerous/marvelous/skillful things."[1] Among those, the superlative one is *mankind*, being both terrible and terrific. The rest of the chorus deploys words associated either with peril or with ingenuity, including a few other polyvalent terms (such as *mēkhanḗ* • *ruse* or *machine*; *krateî* • *having power* or *showing force*).[2] A line in the second antistrophe sums it up by saying that mankind "sometimes moves toward evil, other times toward good" • "tote mèn kakón, állot' ep' esthlòn érpei."[3] These considerations are being opened up by one word ("deiná") that rules over forty lines, with no definite solution in view. Sophocles maintains the semantic bifurcation of *deiná* by exploiting the dyadic structure of the choral ode (where an antistrophe echoes a strophe) and having recourse to paratactic antitheses: "pantopóros: áporos" • "resourceful: resourceless"; "upsípolis: ápolis" • "high on the city: banned from the city."[4] If, while listening to the text, we stick to one region of the semantic specter associated with *deiná*, the next sentence is urging us to move away from one area only and to describe constantly a movement between poles.

Such semantic bistability is akin to what happens with the duck-rabbit in the realm of visual perception. Here, ambiguity or undecidability would not be the best terms, for Sophocles neither advocates grey zones nor relativism, nor does he suspend decision. He is asking us to consider two attractors in the same space (rather than at the same time). I would suggest that the chorus members may have danced alternately by going to the left and to the right (in the line "sometimes moves toward evil, other times toward good," the verb *erpō* means *to go* or *to walk slowly*). The often mimetic aspect of tragic dances sustains this conjecture. Boustrophedon writing—still practiced in classical Athens—was another widespread material structure that could help with spatializing verbal bistability as it occurs in minds. The dynamics of semantics is being performed in this chorus: It requires us to move past the cognitive stability of meaning distribution, if we want to embrace what is being said instead of pinpointing it through reduction.

---

1. Sophocles, *Antigone*, line 334; here and below, my translation from the Greek.
2. See ibid., lines 349, 365.
3. Ibid., line 366.
4. Ibid., lines 359, 370.

2.6.0 In his *Rhetoric*, Aristotle enunciates that verbal art needs to make language sound both "strange" and "foreign" (in keeping with the semantic extension of the original "*xenikón*").[7] Such a duty—much later dubbed in Russian *ostranenie*—appears all the more crucial for poetry, and this duty has often been noted. Readymade sentences and established connections between semantemes are either poetically refurbished or rejected. We habituate ourselves to what has been frequently said and thought. Mental path dependency is being challenged by all levels of defamiliarization: metaphorical networks, unusual word order, morphological alterations, vocables . . . There is not exactly a wealth of experiments on the processing of strangeness in language, and observers commonly try to identify very traditional rhetorical objects, with more or less success. Though available results are quite limited, they tend to confirm that stylistic innovation requires more time and effort to be processed than chunks of standard prose but also—and more interestingly—that thresholds exist. Widespread "metaphors" are conventionalized and treated by the brain like regular lexical elements, but others, perceived to be more "poetic," are treated differently, as integrable though exotic objects.

2.6.1 Sometimes, the foreign tongue of poetry is indeed foreign, like, for centuries, Chinese in Japan, or Sanskrit in vast areas of Southeast Asia.

2.6.2 As for juxtaposition, composition, and hybridization of different languages, they are not modernist inventions. The Greek of Homer and Hesiod is an artificial synthesis of dialects. The choral *stasima* of Greek tragedies, written in a composite dialect, forms the poetry of poetry. Dante incorporates elements of both the North and the South into his Italian. Ezra Pound's *Cantos* use Latin with Old Provençal or Chinese with English. In zones of multilingualism, mixing idioms is most evident.

2.6.3 The musicality of poetry, concreted through alliteration, rhythm, diction, rhymes, and prosodic reorganization, is often underscored by the adjunction of musical instruments and of the singing voice. The "representation networks" of the human mind for language and for music are distinct, but their "resource networks" do overlap.[8] Tecumseh Fitch suggests that this superposition—coupled with other structural commonalities as revealed by poetic practice, whether sung or not—hint at a kind of musical, or primarily prosodic, protolanguage in the ancestry of the *Homo* genus.[9] To me, musicality is a high point on the curve. An intrinsically linguistic construct, poetry bypasses the boundaries of language "as such," through the means of a verbal art. [[12]]

2.7 *Poetry uses imagery, especially in deploying the rhetorical armature of speech.*

2.7.0 The coinage of strong, powerful images may be the most ravishing and subjective aspect of poetry. I see, I hear, I feel what a text evokes. Is this suggestion? From Arthur Rimbaud to imagism and surrealism, modern Western poetry certainly recaptured a picturesque and hallucinatory force that predated it. Now, to literary criticism, images are easy to locate, though difficult to grasp. Their *qualia* is what gives them value; their explanation in theoretical jargon is largely adventitious. [[13]]

12. *The inner musicality of rhyming, prosodic, and metric language in Run D.M.C.'s "Sucker M.C.'s."*

In the "modern" style of hip hop, the emphasis is put on rhyme and on beat structures, reducing melody to a minimum, or even disintegrating it, in favor of rhythmic scratches and the use of a drum machine. In the groundbreaking 1983 "Sucker M.C.'s"—both *ars poetica* and derision of competitors in the tradition of folk-verse jousts—Run and D.M.C. end the song in rapping

[D.M.C.] The rhymes have to make
[Run] A lot of sense
[D.M.C.] You got to know when to start
[Run] When the beats come in.

As Run says in the first part: "Dave cut the record down to the bone | And now they got me rocking on the microphone."[1] Bare-bone rap expresses the inner musicality of rhyming, prosodic, and metric language.

1. All quotes from: "Sucker M.C.'s," B-side of Run-D.M.C., *It's Like That* (New York: Profile, 1983). See the lyrics transcribed in Adam Bradley and Andrew DuBois, eds., *The Anthology of Rap* (New Haven, Conn.: Yale University Press, 2010), 266–268.

13. *Reflexive imagery in Arthur Rimbaud's "After the Flood."*

Arthur Rimbaud's "After the Flood" • "Après le Déluge"[1] usually appears as the first prose poem in the collection *Illuminations*. The whole book *illustrates* Rimbaud's poetics as laid out in his famous 1871 letter to Paul Demeny, having "il faut être *voyant*"[2] • "one has to be a seer" (or "a visionary," or even possibly "flashy") as a motto. "After the Flood" is often read in an allegorical mode—as a comment on the Paris Commune or as a statement on Catholicism—but, in my *view*, its driving force is the power of image. Near the center of the text, "the mourning children looked at the marvelous images" • "les enfants en deuil regardèrent les merveilleuses images," and readers are similarly drawn to imagine and contemplate scenes through the lens of fairy tales, with references to "Blue Beard" • "Barbe-Bleue" or to "the Queen, the Witch" • "la Reine, la Sorcière."[3] Some metaphors harbor the picturesque quality of naïve "engravings" • "gravures" and "marvelous images" coming from children's books or mere "idiotic paintings" • "peintures idiotes,"[4] for example: "a hare . . . said his prayer to the rainbow" • "un lièvre . . . dit sa prière à l'arc-en-ciel";[5] "God's seal blanched the windows" • "le sceau de Dieu blêmit les fenêtres."[6] Images, there, are constantly reflexive. They make us see things; they teach us how to become a seer and alter the limits of perception; they also situate the moving frontier of the seen and the invisible—after all, most critics have to allegorize the poem, for they just do not *see* in "After the Flood" the provincial village waking up after the torrential rains of late winter. But windows are frosted, and we enter a hall of mirrors. The univocal translation of the poetic into its imagery is insufficient, even with Rimbaud's *Illuminations*, for the most vibrant visionary aspects are also opaquely produced through linguistic means that will not so easily self-efface.

---

1. See Rimbaud, *Œuvre-vie* (Paris: Arléa, 1991), 327–328; here and below, my translation from the French.

2. Ibid., 188.

3. Ibid., 327–328.

4. Ibid., 429. In general, one should read "After the Flood" along with the third paragraph of "Alchemy of the Word" in *A Season in Hell.*

5. Ibid., 327.

6. Ibid.

2.7.0.0 Other visionary poets have a tendency to insert pictures into the very fabric of their texts. [[14]]

2.7.1 Poetic images are epiphenomena tied to word constructs—taken as differential recording for the poet's mind in the moment of composition and as cognitive-linguistic infrastructure for the readers.

2.7.1.0 A poetic image is both a prompt for a mental image and *like* an image or, rather, the image of an image. "Simonides names painting 'silent poetry' and poetry 'talking painting,'" Plutarch writes.[10] Speech "graphic energy"[11] might gain in intensity through the poetic, but this can only happen via another, contradictory, densification of the verbal. "Ut pictura poesis,"[12] Horace added, and the first word of the line does matter: *ut* • *as.* [[15]]

2.7.1.1 In the mind, perception is dynamic. It relies on discontinuous pieces of information obtained from our prehension of the world and on their ensuing conjunction. A poetic image is no percept: What is *perceived* of a poem is the whole extent of the signifier, including its rhythmic contours. A poetic image *indexes* the path to imaginary percepts. Moreover, its "tense" is slow and, overall, conscious, in contradistinction with most ordinary sensory perceptions. Finally, the robustness of conjunction tends to be low

14. *Overflowing visions in William Blake's original edition of* America.

In the first edition of *America, a Prophecy,* William Blake adds curly arabesques to his handwriting. He draws coiling tree roots and branches in the margins of the pages. He represents elaborate vines; he paints snakes and dragons with serpentine tails. In the meantime, the "prophecy" describes "a dragon form," a "serpent," an "Orc, wreath'd round the accursed tree," an "Eternal Viper self-renew'd, rolling in clouds . . . | Writhing in pangs of abhorred birth" and that "Heaves in enormous circles."[1] Near the end is a hallucination on "the female spirits of the dead": "Over their pale limbs as a vine when the tender grape appears."[2] The visual *mise en scène* might accomplish more than graphical paralleling, illustrations, or visual counterpoints do. The vision *overflows* from the words themselves and produces the illuminated manuscript, morphed into a kind of supplementary *poem* growing from Blake's own poetic line.

1. William Blake, *America, a Prophecy* (Lambeth: Blake, 1793 [1799?]), 3, 7, 8, 9.
2. Ibid., 15.

15. *The mosaic landscape of Wang Wei's "Deer Enclosure."*

Wang Wei's "Deer Enclosure" (from the "Wang River" cycle) is a perfect example of the perceptual effects reached by classical Chinese poetry.

鹿柴
空 山不見人
但聞人語響
返景入深林
復照青苔上 。
"Lù zhài"
kōng shān bú jiàn rén
dàn wén rén yǎ xiǎng
fǎn jǐng rù shēn lín
fù zhào qīng tái shàng.
•
"Deer Enclosure"
An empty mountain, no man is seen.
Yet, men speaking are heard echoing.
A reflecting light enters the deep forest,
it shines again on the green moss.[1]

The four lines of five characters (and words) gradually compose a scene, through added touches that are in need of combination. Strings of words like "empty mountain not see people | yet hear people speech echo" • 空 山不見人 |但聞人語響 compose a *mosaic* landscape. The scene is visible but interrupted by the isolating character of the idiom as well as by the density of the piece. The picture is there, and not there, depending on where we stand. (The observer's position was, in fact, Horace's chief concern in his *ut pictura poesis*.)

The lack of an explicit subject of enunciation is a widespread trait in classics from the Tang dynasty. Wang Wei's "deer enclosure" could be perceived either from the outside or from within, in which case readers are, in fact, entering the park, hearing the sound of distant people, and seeing the sunlight on the green moss. The "external" understanding assimilates the quatrain with the typical paintings of the literati and considers "Deer Enclosure" as a "painting with sound."[2] Thus, the perceptual space of the text is described by an interpretative position moving between *ekphrasis* (a poem on a painted scenery) and *hypotyposis* (a poem that recreates the impression of "being there"). Even the most "immersive" approach might only *border* the kind of simulation that "virtual reality" grants us. Poetic perception always tends to become too fragmented or metaperceptive as long as we read, for "reading is not seeing." The visionary moment is mainly below and beyond textuality: in imaginative inception and in thoughtful after-effects—that is, when we interrupt or finish our own reading.

EYE	I
DEPICTION	IMMERSION
FRAMING	PARK
EKPHRASIS	HYPOTYPOSIS

Figure 3. Polarities of Wang Wei's "Deer Park" imagery

1. My translation from the Chinese.

2. *Yǒushēng huà* and *wúshēng shī* are two classical Chinese expressions that exactly correspond to Simonides's distinctions between *talking painting* and *silent poetry*. For an overview of this critical tradition in China, see Qian Zhongshu, *Patchwork: Seven Essays on Art and Literature*, trans. Duncan M. Campbell (Leiden: Brill, 2014), 35–40; original text, *Qi zhui ji* (Shanghai: Shanghai guji chu banzhe, 1994), 5–7.

because poetic devices usually morph images and prevent integration. The related paradox is that combination would have to happen at a distance of the text, which cannot fully occur as long as we read or write. We need to absent ourselves from the poem if we want to *see* what it shows. In so doing, we exorcise the demon, while being under its spell. In more secular language, we begin to contemplate the poem, but we stop being *attached* to it. In this *regard*, a poetic image is only "second-order" if seized within the performance of reading, for it incompletely emulates perception.

We do not have to follow the whole trajectory each time. And one could also appropriate the *index* rather than the path or the percepts themselves. This is where literary *thinking* develops. Rimbaud's insistence on deliberate hallucination is about offering to readers not only the controlled and subjective experience of such and such altered state of consciousness but also a quasi-method for sensory delusions that could be applied elsewhere. Surrealists and their heirs certainly promoted similar disorientations, beyond the confines of their own books; some tenets of German romanticism, like those of Novalis, had proposed earlier to modify the human experience of the world by "poeticizing" it.[13]

Mental sensory processing belongs to cognition, so rather than speaking with Gary Lupyan of the "cognitive penetrability of perception," we might prefer to say that ideation and expression are able to percolate into perception. The images of a poem are one complicated example of this phenomenon, potentially happening in three distinct directions: what is the imagined scene, what is consequently seen, what seeing is, ultimately. [[16]]

2.7.2 Tropes pave the way toward imagery.

2.7.2.0 Tropes are cognitive structures, or noetic figures, cutting into the *organon* of language. Tropes are also (meta)cognitive tools, used by the ordered description of discourse. Mental structures may be de jure universal, while taxonomies are, in large part, historically, conceptually, and culturally determined. One can find "metaphors" in speech-acts of all continents; this does not prove them to be a well-defined category that would be common to all human animals—and magically congruent to the consensus of a certain rhetorical tradition at time *t*.

Tropological systems partake in what I call the *cognitive program*, understood as a theoretical project relying *on ordinary protocols of consistence, a double ideal of objectivity and reducibility, a conceptual and deictic use of language, a concern for "the general" or "the universal,"* and a quest for *methodic compression or automaticity*. It absolutely suits rhetoricians (or, for the same reasons, "narratologists" and "metricians") to draw their attention to cognitive *science*, for the latter is the experimental continuation of a strong conceptual position they locally abide by and that still overwhelmingly informs the institution of academia, across all disciplines. There is and always has been a cognitive core in the humanistic endeavor. Traditionalist critics who continue to use the terms of Hellenistic rhetoric while opposing the contemporary study of cognition for literary reading are at an impasse. The taxonomy of tropes is only useful to elucidate some of the cognitive underpinnings of a poem. It is a means, not an end; it is, rather, a beginning. Anchoring poetics in rhetoric (with usually a further reduction to one *Urfigur* or to a simple set) is both ludicrous and self-defeating. Along those lines, poetry could at most claim a *higher* presence of rhetorical devices, since figures are already pervasive in discourse. Even if tropes were *more* abundant in poetry (I am still waiting for

16. *Virgil's fragmented epiphany* (Aeneid, *VI, 268).*

Virgil's line "Ibant obscuri sola sub nocte per umbram" is not only the breathtaking hypallage that manuals of rhetoric have celebrated for centuries. If we read the unfolding of the hexameter, three groups appear:

ibant obscuri	sola sub nocte	per umbram
•		
they went obscure	lonely beneath the night	through the shade.

Thanks to Latin morphology, there is no ambiguity about the syntactic status of *obscuri* (it can only relate to the plural subject of the verb) and none about *sola* (it is an epithet to *the night*). Of course, semantic expectancies are being defied when Aeneas and the Sibyl are said to be obscure and the night to be lonely. There is even a tacit contamination of *sola* by *sol* • *sun*, which introduces a cryptic oxymoron. A good English translation (such as "Obscure they went through the dark beneath the lonely night") is able to retain the main trope, though it disintegrates the very presentation of the sentence elements. Now, word order is extremely significant, for, along with the crossing-over of the hypallage, it participates in the craft of a poetic image that breaks free from logical association or narrative succession: with *sola sub nocte* instead of *sub sola nocte* or *sub nocte sola*; with a paragrammatic *sol* beneath *sola*; with *per umbram* at line's end; with *obscuri* in apposition to the subject and *sola* qualifying *nocte*. Poetic word order is less an expression of grammatical or metrical constraints than an inscription of the imaginative, the cognitive, and the intellective *within time*. No mental process is devoid of timeframe: What we feel to be immediate or instantaneous simply happens very quickly in our nervous system. Our brains usually "see" images (apprehend, analyze, treat, combine stimuli) in under 100 milliseconds and possibly less than twenty. Many other mental operations, even seemingly complicated ones (such as getting a first impression of trust or distrust about someone), are able to take place below the 400 millisecond threshold. Such rapidity largely accounts for the unconscious aspects of basic perception. When—and if—we see Virgil's nightly wanderers at the end of the line, the epiphany takes several seconds to form, up to four or five seconds in the case of formal recitation. Low speed makes us conscious of what we usually ignore—the fragmentation of relevant information. So is the particular synchrony Lessing attributed to "talking images" when he took position in his *Laocoon* on the debate summarized by Horace.

The unexpected sequence of verbally imaged percepts, or the addition of "per umbram," forcing us to return to *obscuri*, *nocte*, and **sol*, weakens the ensuing consolidation of the different features unless we abstract ourselves from the textual level as such and subjectively appropriate the image. This latter operation is both true to the "hallucinatory" qualities of the poem and quite untrue to its deliberately artificial dimension (by threatening to *replace* the emerging and shaky image of the text with a more or less unified picture incorporating extratextual traits borrowed from the memory of the readers). To avoid this dual becoming, literary critics often opt for a rigid description of the rhetorical infrastructure or for impressionistic considerations on what they believe they (or "Virgil," or "the Romans," or "the standard reader") could see.

good numbers), nothing would guarantee their performance to conform to what occurs in readymade parlance. One could conversely suspect that a specific criterion for the poetic enlisting of speech figures includes a powerful rearrangement of the tropological itself.

2.7.2.1 Gilles Fauconnier and Mark Turner's theory of "blending" allows a positive description for the generation of the metaphorical. Whereas it has been accepted for its simplicity and heuristics, the selection of the traits to be "blended" from each mental space is stunningly arbitrary and actually far from its scientific objective. Then, the emphasis on equilibrium tends to conventionalize—and tame—all metaphors or associations. In poems, instability fuels development. Furthermore, taking the rhetorical for the literary is far too exiguous a conception for what we seek to establish. [[17]]

2.7.2.2 The rhetorical armature of a poem is not its armor.

17. *Reentrant metaphorical networks in Paul Celan's "Corona."*

When Paul Celan writes in "Corona" "wir schlafen wie Wein in den Muscheln" • "we're sleeping like wine in the seashells,"[1] complete blending would merely trivialize the *adunaton*. It would not prepare the reader to interpret the additional connections that the poem is making through a series of supplementary comparisons and phonological linkages. The image is difficult enough to "picture," but it is just one in a series of three:

wir lieben einander wie Mohn und Gedächtnis,
wir schlafen wie Wein in den Muscheln,
wie das Meer im Blutstrahl des Mondes
•

we love each other like memory and poppy,
we're sleeping like wine in the seashells,
like the sea in the bloodray of the moon.[2]

A triadic association between *wir, wie, Wein* • *we, like, wine* is constructed through paronomasia. Semantic affinities gather *poppy, memory,* and *sleeping*; intertextual echoes bring together *wine, sea,* and *blood* through the Homeric formula *oînops póntos* • *wine-dark sea*. Are comparisons doubled, or are they fragmented and rearranged? Do they form a jigsaw puzzle? Besides, alliterative structures create another underlying network that furthers supplementary combinations between *Mund* • *mouth, Mohn* • *poppy, Meer* • *sea, Mond* • *moon.*

There, in accordance with its alleged personality in European folklore, the *moon* appears to lie, whereas "the mouth speaks true" • "der Mund redet wahr." It was already clear that standard "blending" would be inoperative: Not only do we have *more* than two spaces to connect, but the poem constantly aims to alter and displace any mental "integration." We also realize that metaphors and comparisons are being made unstable by the other tropes to which they are more or less directly tied. For instance, *Muscheln* • *shells* or, more precisely, *seashells* relates back to the enigmatic *Schale* • *(nut)shell* at the beginning of the poem: "We shell time out of nuts and teach it to move: | time goes back into the shell" • "Wir schälen die Zeit aus den Nüssen und lehren sie gehn: | die Zeit kehrt zurück in die Schale."[3] In retrospect, the seashell is a nutshell, and time a hermit crab—or are they? Likewise, the poem seems both to wander and to go back to itself.

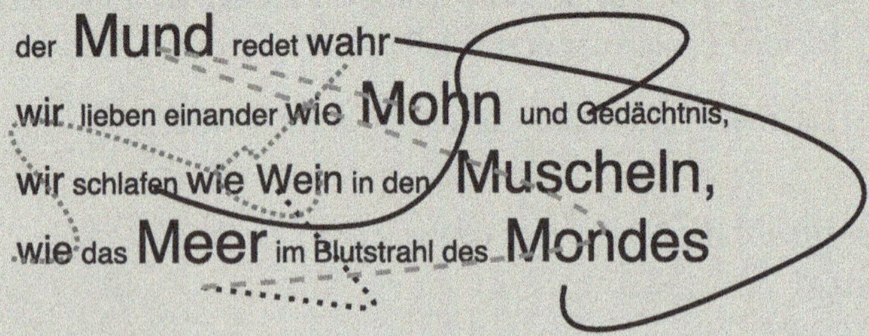

Figure 4. Some metaphorical networks in "Corona"

The circulation of the metaphorical could, in its own turn, be compared with reentrant cortical networks. As Gerald Edelman argues: "Reentry is an ongoing process of recursive signaling among neuronal groups taking place across massively parallel reciprocal fibers that link mapped regions such as those found in the cortex. Reentry is a selectional process occurring in parallel; it differs from feedback, which is instructional and involves an error function that is serially transmitted over a single pathway."[4] To the risk of adding another series of metaphors, then, I would say that Celan's text assembles reentrant metaphorical networks. *Blending* would stay desperately unidimensional and focus on simple communication devices relying on input, output, and feedback. With Celan, we stand at the limits of what is perceivable and tenable, and we intellectively outstretch ourselves as we consider the intricate and moving assemblages of the poem. A corona, after all, is a chain of sonnets commenting and reflecting on one another: The inner movement of the metaphorical is being expanded, against any hope for smooth equilibriums.

---

1. Paul Celan, "Corona," in *Mohn und Gedächtnis: Vorstufen—Textgenese—Endfassung* (Frankfurt: Suhrkamp, 2004), 53; my translation from the German.
2. Ibid.
3. Ibid.
4. Gerard Edelman, "Naturalizing Consciousness," *Proceedings of the National Academy of Sciences of the United States of America* 100, no. 9 (2003): 5521.

2.8 *Poetry is a priori regulated through iterative systems.*

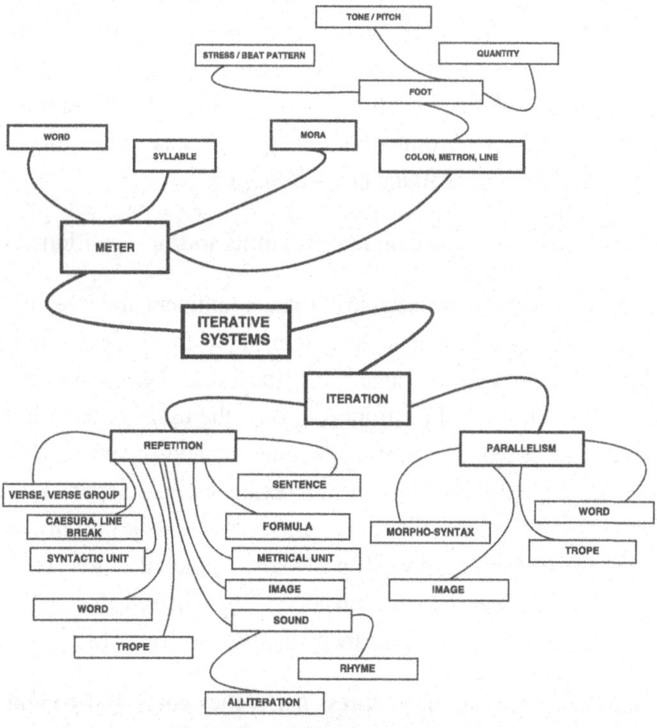

Figure 5. Iterative systems of regulated poetry

2.8.0 "A priori regulation" does not stand for univocal and absolute norms. Rules could be loosely or strictly enforced. They may be common to practitioners and overly binding, determining the number of counted units, the use of some words, or even elements of thematic content (as in seventeenth-century Japanese haiku). They may be recruited "on the fly," in *free* verse, where they constitute evanescent units of organization whose destiny is to vanish as rapidly as they emerge. Ezra Pound's *Cantos* are a masterpiece structured by the unpredictable recourse to ephemeral microregulations of all brands. *Free* verse implies freedom to choose and change the rules "at will." The pace of those shifts is sometimes so rapid and subtle that liberation from templates is actual, without granting complete liberty.

From the pioneering examples of Novalis's *Hymns to the Night* and Aloysius Bertrand's *Gaspard de la nuit* to twentieth-century collections like Lu Xun's *Wild Grass* or Octavio Paz's *Eagle or Sun?*, prose poems—just as free verse, though in a minor key—rely on poetic regulations (iterations, especially). There might be potential exceptions, such as some pieces of Baudelaire's *Paris Spleen*. "Poetic prose" in general often incorporates heterogeneous or free-floating metrical structures and is heavily invested in repetitions of sounds, words, tropes, and motifs (think of François-René de Chateaubriand's *Memoirs*, Emily Brontë's *Wuthering Heights*, or Rainer Maria Rilke's *The Notebooks of Malte Laurids Brigge*).

2.8.1 Iterative systems are based on metrical units and/or repetitions.

2.8.1.0 Measures (or meters) are a staple of many prominent and intercultural systems of poetic regulations, for example, the Arabo-Persian model, with its impressive linguistic, historical, and geographic diversification. In the Indo-European group, the usage of counting syllables and/or feet (determined by quantity and/or stress) is so dominant in poetry that most current textbooks, encyclopedias, or "universal" descriptions still suppose metrical laws to be the only, or the best, ones. In our supposedly postcolonial times, the direct conclusion ("without meter, there is no poetry") is eschewed, though the indirect inference ("poetic lines are metrical") survives. [[18]] [[19]]

2.8.1.1 Measures mark time, they express *tense*; they come and go and come again. Repetition (with and without variation) is an impor-

18. *The historical and the cognitive in metrical systems.*

Metrics, like rhetoric or performance, will be enrolled in a qualification of poetry but not as *scientia scientiarum*. In addition, local revisions are needed. *Moræ*, words, letters, and tones, for instance, could be counted and ordered; lines, rhymes, and stanzas also form superunits. By regarding the variety of items that are being measured, one easily realizes that one solution, in one language and one era, might be locally favored but that meters are mutable and additive. "Mixed" metrical sets (the accentual-syllabic form of ancient Aeolic, Renaissance Spanish, or romantic British lyrics) enforce rules with more insistence, although, overall, any system of measure is able to use other (complementary) standards or sometimes to convert itself. There are deep links between the techniques used by native speakers (as of infancy) for speech segmentation in their mother tongue and the favored type of measures. Most Japanese speakers use *moræ* as tools to locate the beginning and end of words in a flow of speech; French and English speakers will tend to rely on syllables and stresses, respectively. The traditional poetic meters of those three languages are congruent to "native" linguistic strategies.[1]

Concurrently, under certain—social-historical—conditions, a foreign (and reputedly "unnatural") system could be adopted, as when Romans shifted away from their Saturnian stress-based verses and appropriated Greek quantitative metrics, when in Ottoman literature "finger counting" (*parmak hesabı*) poetry receded to the profit of the Arabo-Persian paradigm, or when Xi Murong adopts classical Mongolian versification (based on alliterative lines with parallelism) in her writings in Mandarin. Such shifts remind us that poetic systems, despite their inherent stability, are capable of changing their own rules. Realignment could result from both deliberate strategies and ongoing modification in the structure of language—as was perhaps the case when eighteenth-century Russian poets began considering stress patterns as part of versification, along with the syllabic dimension. More than mere habits, the phonology and prosody of French prevented Baïf's (and his successors') attempts at creating "measured verses" from taking hold: Quantitative patterns may be superimposed to the counting of syllables, but they couldn't replace it entirely in French. In the Latin example, Saturnian verses continued to be used for "inferior" genres, whereas the Greek matrix became the norm for other verbal forms that sought prestige and reclaimed an Athenian ascendancy (e.g., theater, epos, even philosophy, with Lucretius).

---

1. Anne Cutler, *Native Listening: Language Experience and the Recognition of Spoken Words* (Cambridge, Mass.: The MIT Press, 2012).

19. *Poetic feet and binary structures.*

The old word *foot* could be kept for meters made of a determined combination of stressed and unstressed syllables, of long and short vocalic sounds, beats and off-beats, etc. Heavy and short, strong and weak are other parallel terms. The consideration of Asian languages absolutely requires the addition of tone (and/or pitch) to the list of metrical components. Feet seem to be expressed in binary. The triad short-long-overlong of Persian poetry could be an exception, although the overlong is just long if it is found at the end of line, and elsewhere it is equivalent to ⏑—. Siamese or Chinese languages, both having more than two tones, support poetic rules incorporating a dual structure (combinations of *mai ék* and *mai tó* in Thai, of level and deflected, or oblique, tones in Chinese). Meters may tolerate, in some positions, any tone or length (like the final *anceps* of the ancients or the variability of the first or third syllables of each line of a pentasyllabic *lüshi*). Thus, the wide array and complexity of metrical verses based on feet (and their superunits, such as *cola* or *lines*) depend on a very simple—at most ternary, and routinely binary—classification of linguistic phenomena. The basic cognitive plane of poetic regulations is the most evident, and it exhibits the deep tendency of human noetic nonverbal structures to be congruent with the duality of brain lateralization.

tant principle for poetic regulation that operates at many possible levels, from individual phonemes to larger ensembles. The young Gerard Manley Hopkins stated that "the artificial part of poetry . . . reduces itself to the principle of parallelism," an idea that Roman Jakobson expounded.[14] We can claim that the temporal unfolding of the poem is regulated through recurrences, repetitions, and variations based on commonly standardized or more idiosyncratic units. There, categorical differences between *parallelism* and structured *repetition* may be secondary. [[20]]

2.8.2 The iterative systems of poetry are optimized for computation. Conversely, cognitive regulations foster intellection.

2.8.2.0 Through repetition with variation, new, emergent, properties appear. We do not only process incremental changes; we attribute subjective and interpretative values to the whole: We are enthralled, too. Something is solidifying that is more than the sum of its parts and more than a game of permutation. [[21]]

20. *Regulations based on parallelism, accumulation, repetitions.*

Parallelisms of tropes, images, themes, phrases, and syntactic structures are, in the absence of detected meters, what constitute for modern readers the most perceptible regularities of biblical songs. Almost endless cumulation in the encomiastic genre of Xhosa *izibongo* looks like progressive parallelism. In the fifth canto of Vicente Huidobro's *Altazor*, the 190 "free" verses beginning with "Molino" • "Windmill" form a temporal object within the poem and give the image of a potentially transfinite anaphoric variation.[1]

The line breaks (and the internal presence of caesuras) make silence itself the universal object of poetic repetition. Reiteration of sounds is extremely widespread across languages but sometimes loosely structured. Alliterative groups are "on demand" in many European languages. They were essential to the old Germanic or Turkic practices. They are scarce in classical Arabic verses. Rhymes exist in Vietnamese, Chinese, and Swahili but not in ancient Greek or Hebrew. They may be limited to assonance (in very early texts written in Old French), based on vocalic identity and consonantal equivalence (in Tagalog), acceptable in "halves" (in Old Norse), or both internal and at the end of the line (as in the complex pattern of Khmer poetry).

1. Vicente Huidobro, *Altazor*, lines 241–430; my translation from the Spanish.

2.8.2.1 The arithmetic of poetry (counting beats, syllables, *moræ*, lines, stanzas, etc.) participates in a tendency to operate in more than language. Analog numeric cognition tends to activate the intraparietal sulcus in all studied primate species and does not require verbal communication. The strong co-option of nonverbal cognitive abilities for the generation and appreciation of a linguistic object (that is *no* mathematical operation) testifies to the disorientation inherent in poetry and to the insistence on noetic contrasts. If counting elements of discourse while speaking or listening properly makes no sense, it suddenly allows for poetic signification.

2.8.2.2 A further oddity comes from the articulation of metrics with a speech form that simultaneously maximizes semantics—thus defeating the logical principle of a binary (or even ternary) system. While there are only 0s and 1s in an iamb or a trochee, no trochee nor iamb has to express bivalence or be bound by it.

21. *Organized repetition in a Sumerian poem.*

${}^{\text{g̃iš}}$má-kù-gim ${}^{\text{g̃iš}}$má-še-gim
${}^{\text{g̃iš}}$má- ${}^{\text{g̃iš}}$hašhur bal-bal-e-gim
${}^{\text{g̃iš}}$má ukúš-a an-dùl ag-a-gim
${}^{\text{g̃iš}}$má ki-buru$_{14}$ hi-li du$_{8}$-du$_{8}$-a-gim

•

like a boat (full) of silver, like a boat (full) of grain,
like a boat going to deliver apples,
like a boat (laden high with) cucumbers, casting a shade,
like a boat filled with richness at the harvest-place.[1]

So speaks the mythical bird Anzu, who, in a Sumerian poem, is trying to corrupt the human hero Lugalbanda by promising him his magical aid. The profuse and serial imagery functions as an incantation. The poem is suspending its narrative to generate a supplemental impression transcending each individual comparison as well as the dynamics of accumulation. As in charms and curses (representing a genre on their own in the cuneiform corpus), organized repetition aims to be performative: Hypnotic, seductive, exuberant opulence is produced through Anzu's words. More generally, the differential repetition of poetry, while being prima facie algorithmic, is a mechanism that, through *autopoiesis*, overrides the mere transmission of information.

---

1. Jeremy Black, *Reading Sumerian Poetry* (Ithaca, N.Y.: Cornell University Press, 1998), 91–92. Translated by Jeremy Black.

2.8.3 Repetitive, redundant, and rigid behaviors are the basis of human obsessive-compulsive disorders and, more widely, of animal stereotypies. They are seen as soothing or reassuring for the organism that performs them, principally in granting control in a psychological situation of distress and anxiety—even if their consolidation later becomes problematic. They are not exclusively pathological: They seem to be a necessary part of the children's repertoire, and, at the group level, they have connections with many human institutions, as psychoanalysts would argue, and, I would add, with other systematic, costly, and evolutionarily inexplicable behaviors among some other species. [[22]]

2.9 *Poetry is a priori regulated through linguistic reorganization.*

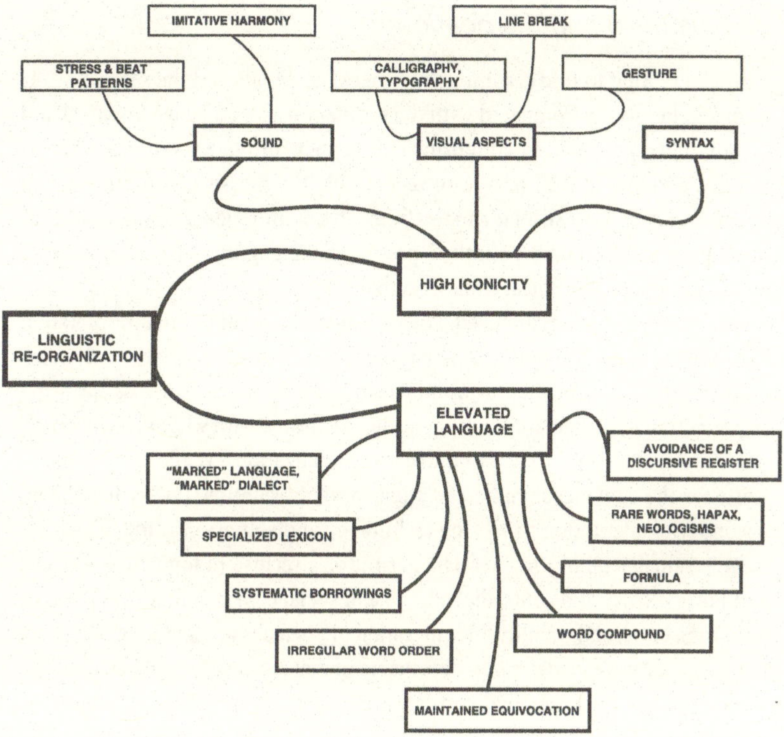

Figure 6. Paths of linguistic reorganization in regulated poetry

2.9.0 In many instances, defamiliarization partakes in regulation. Taxonomic descriptions of poetry rarely mention linguistic reorganization. The phenomenon, far from being absent from the modern European corpus, is perhaps more powerful—or more visibly so—in corpora whose metrics and iterative laws are obscure or relaxed. It is extremely important in many indigenous and aboriginal poems and is systematic in dozens of traditions over the globe. Here too, a combination of rules is to be expected, both internally and externally—with, for instance, vocables or iconic structures being repeated or ingrained in a meter.

2.9.1 Iconicity is a powerful means of poetic regulation.

2.9.1.0 Whereas "imitative harmonies" or rhythmic enactments (speeding, slowing down, walking, galloping) in Greek or Latin epics have been overlooked after Dryden, they resemble a quasi-system. Ono-

22. *The ritual and the poetic.*

It is tempting to find commonalities between rituals and the set of a priori norms in literature. Compared with the ordinary use of language, metrical and iterative poetry exploits repetition and redundancy (through variation), whereas rigidity pertains to the concept of regulation. The massive co-occurrence of poems in religious or secular rituals (from rites of initiation to voodoo celebrations, or from Dionysia to American presidential inaugurations) could indicate an origin of poetry *in* social rituals. So that it would naturally belong to a ceremony, speech would be ritualized. Poems, however, are subject to interpretation in a manner that a coronation or a mass cannot authorize: They are rarely compulsory, and their topics are by no way restricted to concerns such as cleansing or protection—all elements coming in sharp contrast with what Pierre Liénard and Pascal Boyer find to be structuring in ritualization.[1] While synchronicity exists for the audience members of a play or of a recitation, poetry has shown a wonderful adaptation to writing technology and solitary reading, which reinforced the cliché of the poet as a hermit or a recluse (a topos in both Asia and Europe). This too contradicts the role of social cohesion that rites possess. The cross-cultural durability and migration of poems is another practical proof that such texts are *by definition* detachable of any local and ritual background, whereas in-group ceremonial gestures are usually meaningless, ridiculous, or horrid to outsiders.

Are iterative systems in poetry just like rites? Are they a cognitive response to a perceived lack of control or source of distress? Lullabies, after all, are soothing, independently of the lyrics' meaning. The chaos and incomprehensibility of reality and human life would further the need for extreme ordering and the desire to display mastery. The computable mechanics of verse would, then, be the inverted image of the beyond that poetry aims to express. In the meantime, we would feel some emotional solace in the recurrence and variation of what *is* a poem.

1. Pierre Liénard and Pascal Boyer, "Whence Collective Rituals?" *American Anthropologist* 108, no. 4 (2006): 814–827; Pascal Boyer and Pierre Liénard, "Why Ritualized Behavior?" *Behavioral and Brain Sciences* 29 (2006): 595–650.

matopoeias and ideophones abound in traditional Navajo, Hopi, Aztec, or Quechua lyrics, their presence being not ornamental but consubstantial. In fact, by stressing the possibly paradigmatic role of iconicity for poetry, one makes sense of a wealth of regulations from the Americas, Oceania, or Africa. In so doing, one may also rediscover effects that have been marginalized in Europe or Asia. It is worth noticing that the once-influential treatise *On the Composition of Words*—written by Dionysius of Halicarnassus in the first century BCE—expands on *Cratylus* and largely underscores the *mimetic* value of sounds, syllables, and rhythms. "Sound symbolism" never completely disappeared from language, as some recent studies tend to confirm, but poetry always made use of the evocative virtues of phonemes. [[23]] [[24]]

2.9.1.1 Visual iconicity could be extremely relevant in traditions using calligraphy. Concrete poetry is not a late invention within written culture; it is not a *unicum*. The ancient *Greek Anthology* included

23. *Onomatopoeia and calliphony in Humberto Ak'abal.*

Drawing from the usual repertoire of his native Ki'che' language, Humberto Ak'abal, a contemporary indigenist writer from Guatemala, introduces expressive suffixes such as *rapapik* to illustrate the flapping of bird wings or sometimes gathers onomatopoeias in what we could call calliphonic poems, as in "Tormenta" • "Storm" (in Spanish):

Bulun, bulun, bulun, bulun, bulun
Bulun, bulun, bulun, bulun, bulun:
chiplaaaaaaaaaaaaaaa . . . ¶
JIIIIIINNNNNNNNNNNNNN . . .
JIIIIIINNNNNNNNNNNNNN . . . ¶
Mak'ala, mak'ala, mak'ala, mak'ala . . .
Mak'ala, mak'ala, mak'ala, mak'ala . . .[1]

In other parts of the world, Korea, for example, sound iconicity is equally paradigmatic. The refrains of Koryŏ *sogyo* are very frequently onomatopoeic, with Korean pseudowords either imitating the sound of gongs, of drums, of oboes, or making a transition between the articulate voice and instrumental solos. In Amazonia, the Gavião have developed both whistled speech and a speech mode for music instruments, creating songs whose melodies are iconic of language itself.[2]

---

1. Quoted by Rusty Barrett, "Ideophones and (Non-)arbitrariness," *Pragmatics and Society* 5, no. 3 (2014): 413–414.

2. Denny Moore and Julien Meyer, "The Study of Tone and Related Phenomena in an Amazonian Tone Language: The Gavião of Rondônia," *Language Documentation and Conservation* 8 (2014): 613–636.

24. *Mimetic composition in a San song about the fleeing blue crane.*

Putative protomusic, principally made of vocalization, pitch, and humming, could influence sound iconicity in poems and songs. One might speculate that vocables, ideophones, and onomatopoeias are the remnants of a previous art form that has been encapsulated (and altered) within linguistic artifacts. Alternatively, they would look like a differed snapshot of the transitional moment leading from the "musilanguage" Rousseau and others have posited toward verbal prosodic speech. In any case, such "fossils" are necessarily endowed with a largely new function. It is precisely because human language is not—or no longer—essentially mimetic that iconic exceptions may be poetically assembled. Such reorganization implies a vast understanding of the powers of meaningful communication.

The Khoisan people are descendants of the first large group of early *Homo sapiens* to have split from the original population. There are considerable debates on the date of the split, which could have occurred some 100–150,000 or 200–250,000 years BP. At one point, this ethnic group might have been the largest human population, before a significant decline and further intermingling with Bantus. Oral textual practice in Khoisan languages, despite more recent influences and necessary changes, might have kept some very archaic elements. (It has been argued that the Khoisan phonological system retains more traits of ancestral *Homo sapiens* language than other idioms.) The large archive Bleek and Lloyd collected in the late nineteenth century documents tales in the now extinct San language. Many are about the ancient "animal people," who would later become beasts, leaving to the early Bushmen the task to be the only humans. Unsurprisingly, stories or songs are often presented by Bleek's informants as having been taught in the past by the animal people to the San ancestors. Other tales or lyrics are supposed still to be told or sung by other species. The brief song of the fleeing blue crane (*Anthropoides paradiseus*) goes like this:

> ǁkúrru ā !kúïta
> ǁkúrru ā !kúïta
> ǁkúrru ā !kúïta
>
> •
>
> A splinter of stone which is white,
> A splinter of stone which is white,
> A splinter of stone which is white.[1]

Asked to explain the meaning, the informant named ǁkábbo said that "the bird sings about its head, which is something of the shape of a stone knife or splinter, and has white feathers."[2] What the scholar missed, however, is the fact that the original text produces an imitative harmony of the blue crane's call, that a contemporary South African website compares (in English) with "loud, guttural bugle-like notes, 'krraaarrr.'"[3] The poeticity of the brief San lyrics results from a self-referential alignment between evocative onomatopoeias (vocables such as "rrra" or "rrrru" are also woven into other texts) and visual description. Simplicity is deceptive.

1. W. H. I. Bleek and L. C. Lloyd, eds., *Specimens of Bushman Folklore* (London: Allen, 1911), 226–227 [text VI–45: 2157]. Translated by Bleek and Lloyd.

2. Ibid, 227, n. †.

3. See http://www.sanbi.org/creature/blue-crane.

poems in the shape of an egg or an axe blade. In the ninth-century *De laudibus sanctæ crucis*, Rabanus Maurus produced poems where additional, "subliminal" texts would appear through the superimposition of geometrical figures, drawings, or larger letters on the page of the manuscript. Through the move toward specular representation, avant-garde poetry reconnected with a regulation that was historically downplayed in European and meta-European literatures: Completely abandoning meters and marked language, concrete poets take iconicity as a norm. Repetition often co-occurs, from Guillaume Apollinaire's rainfall *calligramme* "Il pleut" to Reinhard Döhl's "Apfel."

2.9.1.2 Along with organized repetition, the iconicity of gesture is of the utmost importance in sign-language poetry.

2.9.1.3 Lineation (realized by typography and respiration or pause) creates the possibility for meaningful enjambments and other comparable effects. [[25]]

2.9.2 Requirements in the alteration (often called "elevation") of language offer another normative set, fulfilled at a lexical and/or a morpho-syntactic level. [[26]] [[27]]

2.10 All regulated poetry having existed and still existing on the globe depends on linguistic reorganization (using high iconicity and language alteration) and/or iterative systems (relying on meters and structuring repetitions). This suggests a common origin and timeline.

25. *Examples of meaningful enjambments or* rejets.

In ancient Greek texts, making sense of the break at lineation is an extant technique. It appears, for instance, in this passage of *The Iliad*:

Tudeḯdeō d' hupèr ỗmon aristeròn ēluth' akōkḕ
égkheos
•
And above the left shoulder of the son of Tydeus came the point of a
spear,[1]

where the sharp end of the lance is ending the line and the spear itself is piercing through the next verse. In the European corpus, we are often in the domain of facultative, rather than paradigmatic, enhancements. Victor Hugo is one of the rare Western modern authors to turn visual iconicity through lineation into—maybe not regulation—but some quasi-system. He goes from very simple *rejets* having mimetic value—like the incipit of his play *Hernani:*

Serait-ce déjà lui? . . . C'est bien à l'escalier
Dérobé
•
Could it be him already? . . . [*a knock at the door*] It is indeed at the secret
Staircase—[2]

to complex dispositions such as:

Ressemblant à la phrase interrompue et sombre
Que l'ouragan, ce bègue errant sur les sommets,
Recommence toujours sans l'achever jamais.
•
Resembling the somber and interrupted phrase
The hurricane, that stutterer astray on summits,
Begins anew without ever achieving it,[3]

where the somber interruption of the sentence is both performed by the verse unit and undone by the enjambment.

I could not identify a poetic form that would systematically implement iconicity via lineation. Still, one could consider that the Japanese *tanka*, if written in one (vertical or horizontal) line encompassing several cola, performs a kind of mandatory "internal enjambment" that becomes mimetic once in phase with depictions of continuity or flow, for example:

あしびきの山鳥の尾のしだり尾のながながし夜をひとりかもねむ

Ashibiki no ⁝ yamadori no o no ⁝ shidari o no ⁝ naganagashi yo o ⁝ hitori kamo nemu

•

Long is the mountain pheasant's tail ⁝ that curves down its flight ⁝ but longer still it seems to me ⁝ left in my lonely plight ⁝ is this unending night.[4]

---

1. Homer, *Iliad*, canto V, lines 16–7; my translation from the Greek.

2. Victor Hugo, *Hernani*, act I, scene 1, lines 1–2; my translation from the French.

3. Victor Hugo, "La Vision d'où est sorti ce livre," in *La légende des siècles*; my translation from the French.

4. Kakinomoto, poem 3 of the collection *Hyakunin-isshu*. In William N. Porter, ed. and trans., *A Hundred Verses from Old Japan* (Oxford: Clarendon, 1909), 3. See Hiroaki Sato, "Lineation of Tanka in English Translation," *Monumenta Nipponica* 42, no. 3 (1987): 347–356. About poetry, iconicity, and cognitive science, see Line Brandt, *The Communicative Mind* (Newcastle: Cambridge Scholars, 2013), 541–594.

26. *Word loans, compounds, and archaisms.*

Loans and borrowings from Pali and Sanskrit have long been the rule in Khmer poetry. Many European languages excluded parts of their lexicon from verses, and they reserved portions of their vocabulary to poetic expression. The French "elevated" lexicon includes *onde* instead of *eau* • *water*, *nuée* in place of *nuage* • *cloud*, and *azur* in lieu of *ciel* • *sky*, all "noble" words being still largely employed by the most aggressive innovators, such as Lautréamont, Stéphane Mallarmé, and André Breton.

Word compounds—*kennings* in Old Norse—have equivalents in Aztec practices and among the Aranda people. Archaisms are mandatory in most, if not all, indigenous songs of Brazil (e.g., Gavião, Suyá) and of the Pacific Ocean. For Alexandre François, who extensively studied the lyrics in the many languages of the Vanuatu Islands, a "taste for archaism" is shared, and, in Motalava for instance, "the texts of songs are so cryptic they are perceived as a totally distinct language."[1] In the Marshall Islands, archaic language (*kajin etto*) and semantic opacity are similarly central and required for poetic songs. The feature is also fundamental in the Hawaiian genre of *kaona*. Far from Oceania, rare terms and neologisms are not incidentally used by many writers of free verse (like Césaire): Along with repetition, they participate in microregulation.

---

1. Alexandre François, *Music of Vanuatu: Celebration and Victories* (2013), 90; https://halshs.archives-ouvertes.fr/halshs-00874941/file/Francois-Stern_2013_Music-of-Vanuatu_MCM_ebook-long_Eng.pdf. See also François, *Araki*, n. 211.

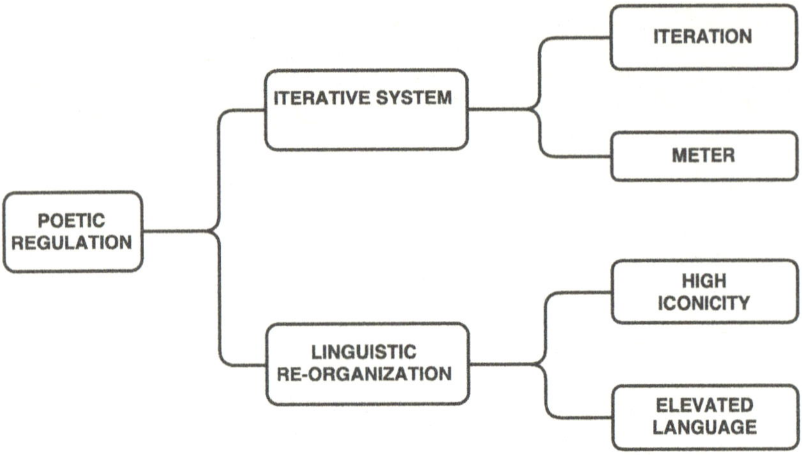

Figure 7. Basic features of regulated poetry

2.10.0 Ubiquitous features among humans might be "inherited" through a combination of genetic and epigenetic transmission. Unless we have to deal with a case of *convergence*, with deep cognitive—and linguistic—structures being co-opted by poetry through "inherited" symbolism. Or maybe we face some kind of coevolution. [[28]]

2.10.1 If dance, music, and vocalization ever existed among humans before the advent of fluent speech, their organization undoubtedly shaped poetic iterative systems. It seems that very few nonhuman animals are able to extract pulse or dance to a tune and that some high-level mastery of vocal communication is needed to "get rhythm." Any antinomy like *body vs. mind* should be repudiated.

2.10.1.0 It might look appealing to fathom an ancestral art form unifying body gestures, dance, music (both vocal and instrumental), and poetry (involving modes of recitation and composition). Separation would occur only locally. Bifurcations would give diversified combinations, leading to the consolidation of potentially coexisting arts, like Western opera or pop music happening in parallel to written poetry or slam, or Hausa poems being either sung or recited. Systems of writing certainly facilitate the relative autono-

27. *Alterations of syntax and morphology.*

Morphological and syntactic conventions that would not be tolerated by native speakers in unmarked usages of their tongues are accepted or even commended in poetic speech. This, I believe, is the most universal feature of regulated poetry, and it is so ubiquitous that it requires no specific illustration. The relaxation of grammatical constraints in poetry is almost exclusively understood as a consequence of metrical and/or musical needs. I disagree. Even in the absence of metrical norms, both words and syntax are structurally altered to become parts of the contrasted *noēsis* of poetry. Some particles in old Quechua (*-y* or *-chu*) were seemingly added as mere marks of "poetic emphasis,"[1] a practice close to the Suyá "song words."[2] Against Ariphrades, an author of comedies who mocked the irregular order of sentences in tragedies, Aristotle noticed in his *Poetics* that the "displacement of words" and the poetic flexibility of grammar have the virtue of creating "the nonidiomatic."[3] This necessary inflexion of the idiom is maintained, maybe expanded, by requirements of meters or musical beats, but it is autonomous. It bears the mark of the vast linguistic reorganization that poems bring forth.

1. Jean-Philippe Husson, *La poésie quechua dans la Chronique de Felipe Waman Puma de Ayala: de l'art lyrique de cour aux chants et danses populaires* (Paris: L'Harmattan, 1985), 179, 333–337.

2. Anthony Seeger, *Why Suyá Sing* (New York: Cambridge University Press, 1987), 45.

3. Aristotle, *Poetics*, 22: 1458b. My translation from the Greek.

mization of verbal poetry. But I would be suspicious of any narrative of unity-and-fragmentation. And I'd seriously doubt any linear (and irreversible) progressions, for new associations can and will emerge between different expressive means. Rather than being a mythical point of departure, the potentially unified art form may have concatenated previously distinct symbolic genres. Unity could be local too.

2.10.1.1 Prosody, musicality, meter, repetition, symmetry, rhythm, and iconicity are all cognitive phenomena intersecting with language, both predating it and being modified by it. Regulated poetry appears when all those aspects are skillfully immersed within discourse and when the powers and pitfalls of human speech are perceived and

28. *Further conjectures on the longstanding existence of poetry.*

By mapping the four basic nomological traits, we cannot find evidence for any of those to be a "later invention." In particular, Aboriginal Australian populations—thought to descend from one of the earliest successful migrations out of the original continent (40–80,000 years BP)—make use of all four features in their traditional poetry. The oldest written records (third millennium BCE) are in Egyptian, Sumerian, and Akkadian. Both Egyptian and Akkadian poetry display repetition and parallelism as well as elevated language (in Akkadian, only the Babylonian dialect is used in poetry, not Assyrian). The virtual universality of the main directions for regulation strongly supports the conjecture about the longstanding existence of poetry. In an evolutionary perspective, then, poetic rules as we know them could have been with humans *before* the great dispersion out of Africa, possibly 120,000 years ago, and 60,000 years ago at the very latest. Structured iterations derive from cognitive structures that are supposedly adaptive, while speech potentialities are just inherent in human verbal language (and mostly derive from granularity or defects). Then, one could assume that regulated poetry *either* began as a more or less random byproduct of some language traits, before being consolidated through an iterative system (old progressive hypothesis), *or* emerged from cognitive structures that merely happened to be "trapped" in discursive—and surface—realizations (new positivistic hypothesis). One could propose that nomological poetry stemmed from the percolation of virtually preexisting mental systems of ordering with the reuse of unintended effects of language specificities. Both cognitive ordering and linguistic characteristics are consubstantial with *Homo symbolicus*.

Regulations are deduced properties of the cognitive architecture: They pertain to a timeline that seems quasi-static, given the human lifespan. Now, *particular* poetic rules are situated historically, either on the *longue durée* or on a more eventful and accelerated pace. Most European popular songs have continuously used rhymes and refrains since at least the Middle Ages; the hendecasyllable resurfaces regularly, in the ancient Eolic islands, in medieval Italy, in Goethe's lyric; some contemporary Arabic authors still adopt the sixth-century codification of *'arūḍ*. In contrast, other devices are more short lived: the newly specific emphasis on visual iconicity that informed the concrete poetry movement blooms internationally in the 1950s–1960s before fading away; overlong syllabic French verses (counting more than twelve syllables) are mainly a twentieth-century experiment; in Europe, the genre of rhymed epistles is largely passé. The historical anchorage is also apparent in the social, political, and technical environments that discourage or favor poetic regulations. The intricate rules of classical Amharic, Greek, Chinese, or Sanskrit poetry depend on well-built systems of conservation and transmission, high symbolic value attributed to poetry, political protection and stability, and a propitious organization of social time and space. An egalitarian nomadic group with little means of subsistence, no writing, and little separation of status and function would not provide the milieu one finds in a centralized empire invested in the production of a scholarly caste or in a network of cities whose economy relies on agriculture, exchanges with other nations, and work provided by slaves. Thus, neither the cognitive nor the intellective are impervious to the social-historical.[1] Despite all the vicissitudes of the social-historical and the diversity of cultures, the apparent antiquity and ubiquity of the four main parameters for regulated poetry indicates that poetic oeuvres are, as music and architecture, a longstanding staple of the human experience, since at least the primeval *Homo sapiens* society.

1. I say it again, *Poetry and Mind* is not negating *The Empire of Language*: Social, historical, and political formations do intersect with the way we speak, act, and think. But, depending on the scholarly goals we pursue, we do not always need to treat equally all dimensions of the same phenomenon. In my 2016 *Refusal of Politics*, I also show how, from its extremities, the political could be undone: This experience is comparable to the intellective override of cognition. Literature, then, is not "apolitical" in the banal sense of the term (that is: cut from the social-historical), but it may open up a breach within the political edifice.

mobilized. In all likelihood, the rudiments of this art materialized at least several dozens of millennia ago. All verbal animals having the ability to organize the two most basic features of iteration and speech reorganization would be able to express or experience poetry. "The singing Neanderthal,"[15] if there were any, may well have been a bard too.

2.10.2 Origin, after all, is overrated. The mental experience of poetry is neither severed from archeology nor hostile to history. But it has more to offer than a date of birth and a chronology.

2.11 *Poetry tends to exceed its own algorithms.*

2.11.0 The two basic features of poetic regulations *frame* cognition differently. It is through an exceptional reautomation of language—and of its underlying noetic structures—that higher-order deautomation is to be achieved.

2.11.1 The "algorithmic" dimension of poetry is dual. One lies at the perceptual level of stimulus processing; the other deals with the "writing program" of a piece constrained by its predictable conventions (including versification) and inner dynamics.

2.11.1.0 Percepts are normally treated by the algorithmic brain; there is little reason to presume an exception for the sound, voice, and music of poetry. When we hear the alternations of short and long vowels, nonrandom sequences are acknowledged, creating anticipation for the other accents of the line. The particular domain of processing regulated verses has been unevenly explored so far, but we can make many inferences, since very general properties of the central nervous system are probably at work here. Of course, poetic structures are not fully contingent historically, and the human genius needs to "make do," according to its capacities and capabilities. For instance, the short-term memory in our brains seems to condition strictly the number of "information units" we can "hold" together. [[29]]

2.11.1.1 Readers anticipate textual events on the basis of their comprehension of the fixed form. The Malay listeners at a *pantun* recitation expect the sounds of the words at line ends to reappear, and they guess that the second part of the stanza will echo the first half, both phonetically and thematically. The poetics of "wax and gold" used in Ethiopia encourage Amharic readers to look for the pivotal word that will allow the *double entendre* of the text.

Theoretically, though not presently, algorithmic comprehension could be formalized and computed by artificial intelligence. Brains are currently described as "predictive machines." Even before the beginning of a verbal interaction between two individuals, their nervous systems are computing information, based on what they know, and are anticipating probable segments of conversation and parts of sentences. Common knowledge is based on features of the physical world, similar neural architectures, past social and cultural experience, memory, intellectual training, familiarity between people, and so on. Anticipating the second half of a story or the hidden top of a picture is the kind of predictions we make all the time. Poems, in particular highly regulated ones, include a *program* that knowledgeable readers can "predict." Readers with a vast memory of poetry are usually less satisfied by texts their minds

29. *Mental storage capacity and caesuras.*

Reuven Tsur sought to show that cognitive limitations shape what I would call the technical range of the poetic. In 1956, George Miller spoke of "the magical number 7, ±2"[1] to situate the upper boundary of the working capacity of *Homo sapiens*'s memory. Tsur and others connected this observation with the length of metrical lines and the seemingly universal phenomenon of caesura.[2] Contemporary psychologists revised their assessment of the storage capacity for human memory, reducing the highest number to 5 or even 4 (±1), while substituting *chunks* of compressed information to "items" as such—seven mental elements being often compressible, through redundancy, to a number inferior to seven.[3] Caesuras, in this view, are optional pauses that *could* be marked, in order to allow the mental processing of rhythmic patterns, and *could* coincide with syntax or become meaningful. The mechanics of perception is useful for situating the pitfalls of radical historicism, for underlining why similar patterns are to be found across cultures, for locating potentially universal features, for aligning the asemantic mental processing of literature with other facts of perception. It might also serve, perhaps more paradoxically, to solve longstanding philological controversies, like the debate on Homer's dactylic hexameter and the function of feet, cola, and caesuras therein.

1. George A. Miller, "The Magical Number Seven, ±2," *Psychological Review* 63, no. 2 (1956): 81–97.

2. See Reuven Tsur, *Toward a Theory of Cognitive Poetics* (Amsterdam: North-Holland, 1992), 172; Mikhail Gasparov, *A History of European Versification* (Oxford: Clarendon, 1996), 8.

3. Nelson Cowan, "The Magical Mystery Four," *Current Directions in Psychological Science* 19, no. 1 (2010): 51–57, for an overview; Fabien Mathy and Jacob Feldman, "What's Magic About Magic Numbers?" *Cognition* 122, no. 3 (2012): 346–352.

are able largely to "foresee." At the same time, the general process of defamiliarization of poetry contributes to a much more singular project—let us call it a *programme*—that is much more difficult (and, often, practically impossible) to anticipate. [[30]]

2.11.2 The moment one considers a regulated line as a predetermined template that is to be realized, one admits the operation of a core algorithm in poetry. From Chomskyan linguistics to literary movements like Oulipo, verse generation, as well as scanning, have been described—implicitly or explicitly—as algorithmic tasks. Even the old-school taxonomy of regulated verses relies on the same

30. *Program and programme in Luis de Góngora's "On the Deceitful Brevity of Life."*

De la brevedad engañosa de la vida
Menos solicitó veloz saeta
destinada señal, que mordió aguda . . .

•

On the deceitful brevity of life
Less swiftly did the arrow seek
the destined mark it sharply bit . . .[1]

Reading the title and the first few lines of Góngora's "On the Deceitful Brevity of Life" • "De la brevedad engañosa de la vida," there are many aspects of the poem I can predict right away. Even without any external information about the author, my brain (or a computer software) can readily detect the Spanish language of the text—which comes with syntactic and lexical expectancies. I identify hendecasyllables at the onset and can bet this verse form will be kept throughout the poem, without being at first able to rule out the recourse to other meters. If I am told in advance that this is a sonnet, then, with the help of my "European memory," I could predict that the first two stanzas will use the two rhymes appearing in the quote above. Since I imagine that the title is giving me some clue about content—and by amalgamating what I remember of the Spanish Golden Age and its relation to the European Renaissance and baroque—I can promptly relate this sonnet to topoi like *tempus fugit* or *vanitas*. If the emphasis is on the passing on time, I'll look for time units—we'll actually find "las horas" • "the hours," "los días" • "the days," "los años" • "the years" at the end of the second tercet—and for references to ways of counting hours—which I will not discover, unless the "arrow" of the beginning obliquely refers to a clock or a sundial. If the focus is on the vanity of human life, I'll expect the presence of motifs like those represented in still lifes (a skull, a sandglass), which happen to be absent. Regarding the composition of the text, I imagine that the initial notion of the poem will first be developed and explained in the quatrains: I am prepared to find a *pointe*, a *conceit*, a *reversal*, or some striking formula in the last lines. Finally, the inner dynamics or "logic" of the speech form appears to prevent sudden thematic or stylistic changes. All those aspects could be somehow anticipated, which implies, of course, that predictions could be defeated (*desinit in piscem*). Still, the end is somehow familiar, with an *I* telling a *you*:

Mal te perdonáran a ti las horas;
las horas que limando están los días,
los días que royendo están los años.

•

You won't be well forgiven by the hours;
the hours that are eroding the days,
the days that are gnawing the years.

Let us suppose that, with enough patience and technological advancement, this multilayered *Erwartungshorizont* could be simulated by a nonhuman machine and could even include partial revisions based on the accumulation of new data, in a Bayesian perspective. We would have located the *program* of the poem.

Now, its *program* does not necessarily enclose its *programme.* Not only is life's brevity "deceitful," but the title that says so also deceives the readers. In the text, *brevity* is metaphorically expressed, and *life* is mediately mentioned as well (with, for instance, "nuestra edad" • "our age"); still, the terms themselves are missing. Conversely, the third noun of the title phrase is related to "engaños" • "deceits," at the end of line 11, where it rhymes with the final "años" • "years." Graphically, then, *years* • *años* are contained within *deceits* • *engaños*—or, rather, years, as a metonymy of time, are what's left of the illusion of life.

The anadiploses of the last tercet ("las horas | las horas," "los días | los días") were possible, though not likely, and not especially expected. They form the additional signature of a very well-structured sonnet whose elements are joined by doubling. After the first six lines, each new argumentative component is tied to the previous one by retrospective considerations. The recursive trope of the last lines is a rhetorical linkage that accompanies the demonstration of the text. The final image is even more striking, with the fabric of the days that are becoming threadbare ("limando" • "eroding") because of the hours and the days that years are gnawing. The erosion of time is poetically performed, when the *engañosa* of the title is shortened to *engaños,* which is further reduced to *años.* This is the last word of the sonnet: It will not be uttered again, as if it had dissolved into silence. While our cognitive algorithms could recover a sensible portion of the sonnet's *program*, its *poetic programme* would not be *pre*dicted by our minds in any robust way. Technophile enthusiasts might state that a big-data analysis of baroque sonnets would allow a computer to anticipate such effects. I do not think so (this is an open challenge). At most, a software application might suggest the occurrence of *años* as a rhyme after *engaños* and relate this to paragrams in general and to the particular title—but both the motivation and signification of such *literal erosion* would still be lacking. Were I proven wrong, and were a machine able to make a relevant guess thanks to massive data mining, I'd continue to doubt that a human mind would predict (and not interpret retroactively) this effect while *reading*, and without even having the storage capacities contemporary networks of computers do. As for the writer himself, Góngora certainly never "predicted" the end of this piece: It either came to him through the performance of writing (via unconscious material processes, conscious selection, and consolidation, all becoming a programme in retrospect), or it was a point of departure for composition, based on a reflexive consideration about the openness and opacity of human language.

1. Sonnet included in Luis de Góngora, *Selected Poems* (Chicago: University of Chicago Press, 2007), 100–102; my translation from the Spanish.

kind of dogma. Metrics emphasize the machinery of the verse and show principles of substitutions that could be structurally automated. Yet, *rules are implemented in poetry in order to generate irregularities.* "Exceptions" or "imperfections" are the goal—a goal only reached through the creation and maintenance of some novel "order" to be transgressed. This is where nomological poetry *tends* to *exceed* (without forgetting or escaping) its own algorithm. [[31]]

2.11.2.0 Unexceptional poetry is *flatus vocis.*

2.11.2.1 "Computer-generated poetry" outsources parts of the composition process to a nonhuman mind. "Computer-assisted poetry" might be a more appropriate label, for, so far, the writing of the software is still done by "wet brains." When in *#!* Nick Montfort publishes the code with the generated poem on the opposite page, he is juxtaposing the "template" with the "verbal mapping" (as if iambs were to be printed along with their possible patterns and laws of derivation). Do exceptions occur? Regular computers would only exceed their algorithms if they were programmed to do so, in which case they would no longer exceed their (meta)program. By selecting the pieces he collects, Montfort could, in a sense, go beyond automated generation, and we, as readers, might grant signification through interpretation—if we're not killed by boredom before this.

2.11.2.2 Henri Meschonnic is wholly justified to write that in poetry, "rhythm exceeds measure" • "le rythme dépasse la mesure."[16] This is exactly what happens in metrical lines. But claiming that "rhythm is the very organization of meaning in speech"[17] is misleading: What bypasses cognitive regularity can only emerge from the defection of organized thought. Then, in practice, Meschonnic

31. *Algorithmic approaches to the dactylic hexameter.*

The traditional rendition of the classical dactylic hexameter, dating back to Hephaestion's Hellenistic textbook, basically tells us that the mind (of the poet, of the reader) is encapsulating discourse in alternate patterns of long and short syllables, according to a model of the type

–⏖ ⁝ –⏖ ⁝ –⏖ ⁝ –⏖ ⁝ –⏖ ⁝ –⏓ |[1]

On the basis of specific rules on length or additional norms (on caesura, for instance) and devices (formulas), once given a vocabulary set constrained by morpho-syntax and spelling (with more degrees of freedom on both counts than in ordinary language), the brain of the poet would compute the appropriate series of words. In the meantime, the listener undoubtedly anticipates rhythm—often yielding the "right" prediction but often being defeated by the selected string of short and long vowels. Statistics compiled on *The Iliad* and *The Odyssey* show that lines of the sort –⏑⏑ ⁝ –⏑⏑ ⁝ –⏑⏑ ⁝ –⏑⏑ ⁝ –⏑⏑ ⁝ –– | account for roughly 19 percent of the text, while –– ⁝ –– ⁝ –– ⁝ –– ⁝ –– ⁝ –– | is pretty scarce (≃0.02 percent).

In 1677, John Peter published a treatise entitled *Artificial Versifying*, designing a largely automated "*Rule* of *Operation*"[2] (that is, an algorithm) mining a lexical database in Latin and generating dactylic hexameters such as "Tristia fata tibi producunt sidera prava" • "Your sad fate brings forth pernicious stars."[3] In 1845, John Clark finished building a machine producing similar lines (but in one minute, and to the tune of the British national anthem), among which is "Horrida sponsa reis promittunt tempora densa" • "The horrid spouses of things promise dense times."[4] Both Peter and Clark cut corners: Their lines are six words long, and they repeat a small set of predetermined metrical structures, which severely limits the power of their endeavors. All algorithmic descriptions are not born equal.

The contemporary metrics of Nigel Fabb and Morris Halle, with its different levels and "grids," is full of strange ad hoc interventions in the supposedly automatic generation of the text. Moving from one grid line to the next requires many subaltern "rules" that magically appear to "repair" any problem that could have occurred in the examination of specific textual fragments. Those repairs look a lot like haphazard fixes to a wanting theory. The "head of line" this method uncovers is often inoperative, as has been established by several commentators, or is a mere preconception. At most, the Fabb-Halle hypothesis provides us with a semiautomatic—and ultimately messy—description, leaving us with *bricolage* in the guise of algorithm.

Other attempts at generative metrics postulate abstract periodic templates, with words being mapped on the template. Realists acknowledge the discrepancy between actual verses and ideal patterns, usually speaking of "imperfect" mapping. The difficulty here is, once again, an obsession with syntax, coupled with the repetition of Shannon's communication diagrams: "Imperfections" are presented as *noise*—and what matters is the algorithmic law of derivation. Yet, the aim is to create acceptable exceptions through the installation of constraints. The "generative algorithm" of metrical lines is just a reautomation of the poetic deautomation of language that prepares some further deautomation at the level of the verse.

---

1. ⏖ is for either two short or one long (two short being more expected, since a dactyl is –⏕; ⏓ is for either a short or a long (a long being more expected). The fifth foot is almost always a dactyl. There are lots of other intricacies I am omitting here.

2. John Peter, *Artificial Versifying* (London: s.n. 1677), 7.

3. Ibid, 11; my translation from the Latin.

4. See *Littell's Living Age* 7 (1845): 214–215; my translation from the Latin. Clark's machine, the Eureka, will supposedly be soon restored to working condition.

never shows how the rhythmical *exceeds* the metrical, for he always *opposes* the two and just *neutralizes* the algorithmic.

2.11.2.3 In the diction of poetry, "regular" algorithms—within the "software" of versification—are done, or half-done, or undone. We like all aspects together. There may be as much joy and satisfaction in perceiving that the putative "template" is realized than in hearing it is not. The art lies both in the program *and* in its defection. [[32]]

2.11.3 Since "critical reading practices already contain elements of the algorithmic," why not plead in favor of "algorithmic criticism?"[18] Because we might see in the latter expression something like a tired gimmick, one tied to the phrase of the digital (or "computational") "revolution" that is supposedly "liberating" the human race from bondage. Because we do not believe in the mystical agency of the result and cannot condone statements like "The data confirm that *x*." Because, if algorithms are indispensable *elements* of critical thinking, using computerized means can make some of our conjectures and findings more robust, but *that is all*. Because the temptation to *confine* the literary to the rhetorical and the generic, or fiction to storytelling, or the poetic to the metrical, or creation to algorithms has been with us for centuries (in the very heart of "the humanities"). This temptation should be fought against today as it has been fought against before. [[33]]

32. *The interplay of definition and diction in French regulated poetry.*

The French system of regulated verse is relatively simple, even poor: Since the early Middle Ages, each line is simply *defined* by a number of syllables. The decasyllable and the alexandrine have additional rules for caesura. Supplementary laws for rhymes (including an alternation of "feminine" and "masculine" line ends) have been gradually devised, reaching some stability from the Renaissance to the last century, but we may theoretically set them aside by envisioning each verse as a potential monostich. A well-formed line, then, is a relatively straightforward matter, as soon as one agrees on the way to count syllables. In Old French, the production of syllables was generally unambiguous, but the status of the *e muet* [ə] (the French schwa), not always realized in common oral language since at least the sixteenth century, became a difficulty. The major convention is to pronounce every [ə] in a line, if followed by a consonant, with the possible exception of some grammatical morphemes (e.g., in the suffix *-aient*, used to mark in verb conjugation a third-person plural in the imperfect past tense, the *e* is "mute") and some words with a final *e*. In the Renaissance, an *e* at the end of a verse is realized as well, though this supernumerary syllable is not "counted." This latter practice probably disappears in the seventeenth century or so. An exception is in music—both classical and folk music—where most or all final *e*'s tended to be uttered, which was even true of rock songs until the 1980s.

The simplicity of metrics in French (compared, for instance, with Sanskrit, Arabic, or English) is undeniable. The problem is that generations of scholars—and sometimes poets—have neglected the *diction* of the French verse. If the syllabic "generation" is purely algorithmic, each line relies on the moving stress pattern, on the perceived duration of each syllable, on the changing tones of the phrase. (Some tenacious legends claim that the French language has no stress or that stresses always fall on the last syllable of each word. The first claim is inept. The second is accurate only if one considers a language as a collection of single words. In French, stress patterns are not as fixed as in German or English but are flexible and depend on word groups and semantics.) In the proven absence of isochrony, syllabic "length" is linked to the nature of vocalic sounds and to pragmatic aspects; intonation could be conventionalized; stresses, except those at the end of a line, do *not* depend on syllable counting. In short, the *definition* of a French verse is numerical; its *diction* is not. The interplay of definition and diction is the root of French "counted" poetry. In particular, the tension between the immobility of the count and the mobility of the stress is a powerful means. It is reassuring to see that such aspects are understood by a wide variety of theoreticians, from Antoine Fouquelin's 1557 *La rhetorique françoise* and Bénigne de Bacilly's 1671 *Traité de la méthode* to Georges Lote's 1929 pioneering research in poetry using acoustic spectra and the more recent work of Henri Meschonnic. But it is fair to say that, in their majority, critics are simply unaware of the basic qualities of French lines.

33. *Installation and defection of the algorithmic in Jean Racine's alexandrine* (Phèdre, *act I*).

Jean Racine's tragedies operate within a mostly periodic and melodic distribution of stresses in each line. Racine's standard alexandrine bears a major stress at caesura and at the end of the line, with two minor stresses, often on the third and ninth syllables. This normativity conforms with the political aesthetics of absolute monarchy. It also possesses a hypnotic, ritualized, character. A multitude of variations, however, shift the place of accents: Once several verses in a row show the same pattern, they generally give way to other structures, in an unexpected fashion (for *how* and *when*). Strong, abrupt, and basically improbable sequences of stressed and unstressed syllables also occur here and there. The unfortunately widespread pronunciation of Racine's text on stage, systematically assimilating *all* lines to 1 2 3 4 5 **6** 7 8 9 10 11 **12**, creates an unbearable monotony that rehashes the template while reducing the diction of the verse to the mapping of its definition.

One could also suppose that a spectator who discovers the text is processing the data—here the stress patterns—and that her mind uses a kind of "learning algorithm" to anticipate the rhythmic qualities of the next line, constantly revising her hypothesis on the basis of prior results. The distribution of stresses is far from random, so our spectator will quickly have expectations, which will be met. We take for our purpose the first two scenes of Racine's *Phèdre*. In this corpus, around 60 percent of the lines have a major stress on their sixth and twelfth positions as well as a minor stress on the ninth syllable, conforming to the structure:

n **6** 9 **12** (n<5).

The overall stress positions in each hemistich (especially if disregarding the accent intensity) also appear to be quite symmetrical: The last syllable of each part of the alexandrine is almost always stressed, whereas the penultimate is never marked, the probability for the second syllable of each hemistich to be stressed is statistically similar, etc.

Such is the background that makes us even more aware of any violation of the norm, as evidenced in the third scene of the first act and the entrance of Phèdre on stage. There, passion is the rhythm springing from the meter. The confusion of the main character, who is lovesick for her son-in-law and reveals the secret of her forbidden feelings to her confidant, spreads to the music of the verse. In divergence with data-based computation, stresses and arithmetical subunits no longer coincide. When Phèdre and her maid Œnone share the same line, the illusion of a regular ternary structure instantly vanishes, as in this alexandrine in three parts:

PHEDRE. **J'aime** . . . ŒNONE. Qui? PHEDRE. Tu connois ce Fils de l'Ama**zone.**
1 2 3 4 5 6 7 8 9 10 11 **12**
•
PHEDRE. I love . . . ŒNONE. Whom? PHEDRE. You know that Son of the Amazon.[1]

The previous line, without any external interruption, was already using the aposiopesis after "J'aime . . ." • "I love . . . ," as well as both alliteration and parataxis, to alter the standard diction that is otherwise established as of the first scene of the same play:

J'aime . . . à ce nom fatal je tremble, je fris**sonne** [diction A]
1 2 3 4 5 6 7 8 9 10 11 **12**
J'aime . . . à ce nom fatal je tremble, je fris**sonne** [diction B]
1 2 3 4 5 6 7 8 9 10 11 **12**
•
I love . . . to this fatal name, I am trembling, I am shaking.[2]

The realization of the alexandrine is not decided once and for all: The absence of comma after "fatal" invites us to skip the caesura and displace the minor accent to "tremble," which is about to be duplicated with "frissonne." Then, verses such as

O haine de Venus ! O fatale co**lere** !
1 2 3 4 5 6 7 8 9 10 11 **12**
•
O Venus's hatred! O fatal wrath![3]

are very unlikely, largely unpredictable, and at odds with either the iterations of the model or a statistically based prediction. Arguing, as Mikhail Gasparov does, that "the stress structure of both hemistiches in French *alexandrine* is determined only by the rhythmical vocabulary of the French language and nothing else"[4] is awfully shortsighted: The writer is choosing the words to consolidate or disrupt the dominant rhythm of his poem. As a matter of fact, Gasparov, who worked after Kolmogorov on probabilities and verse formation, always assumes the presence of a stress on the sixth and the twelfth syllable of each alexandrine when he scans the text: Thus, his computational bias is *fabricating* the data, just as Fabb and Halle do when they posit that the "projecting syllable" of an alexandrine is always right before caesura.

In addition to ellipsis and interruption, to the mimetic displacement of the regularized pattern, the oral underscore of poetic devices can modify the schema and merely enrapture.

Ariane ma **Sœur** ! De quel amour blessée,
Vous mour**ustes** aux bords où vous **fustes** laissée !
1 2 3 4 5 **6** 7 8 9 10 11 **12**
1 2 3 4 5 6 7 8 **9** 10 11 12

Ariadne, Sister mine! By what love you were harmed
To die on the shores you'd been left at![5]

is a much more powerful and gripping diction than a flat "Vous mourustes aux **bords** où vous fustes laiss**ée** !" The emphasis on the internal rhyme in [y:t] inverts the dominant positions of major and minor stresses, which is mirrored by unconventional intonation (descending at both caesura and end line). The very unusual place of a *minor* stress on the twelfth syllable allows a performance ending with a whisper or a sigh. It resonates with the depiction of Phèdre as a weak, dying, and breathless figure.

1. Jean Racine, *Phèdre*, line 262; my translation from the French. In the quotes, I am keeping both the spelling and the punctuation of the original ed.: Racine, *Phedre et Hippolyte* (Paris, Barbin: 1677).

2. Ibid., line 261.

3. Ibid., line 249.

4. Mikhail L. Gasparov, "A Probability Model of Verse (English, Latin, French, Italian, Spanish, Portuguese)," *Style* 21, no. 3 (1987): 334.

5. Racine, *Phèdre*, lines 253–254.

2.11.4 All this also leaves completely open the question of the algorithm that produces the algorithm (the algorithm that would have "computed" the genre of the sonnet at the cosmopolitan court of Frederick II in thirteenth-century Sicily or the one that would have allowed Gertrude Stein to come up with her own). Is it nondeterministic? Is there any such algorithm? [[34]]

2.11.5 The poetic is incommensurable with the algorithmic that nonetheless allows it.

2.12 *Poetry is complex and highly incompressible.*

2.12.0 While the core unexpectedness of poetic texts needs to be appreciated in contrast with normativity, it defeats in advance any attempt to contain it completely. To borrow a concept from information science and mathematics, poems are highly *complex*. Very repeti-

34. *Poiēsis and the uncomputable.*

The nonreductive interrelation of the algorithmic and the poetic could appear to transpose, by way of analogy, the possible discrepancy between *P* and *NP* in computer science. *P* is the class of decision problems solvable by a Turing machine in a deterministic way and in polynomial time; in *NP*, solutions are to be found in nondeterministic polynomial time. Following Alan Cobham's original suggestions, it is often considered that polynomial time corresponds, in rough terms, to "feasible" or "easy" solutions. Most scientists now tend to assume the inequality of *P* and *NP*, but, so far, nobody has been able to prove or disprove the conjecture. If $P \neq NP$, we may have problems that cannot be solved through a tractable series of algorithms, even if their solution(s), when found by another method, are apt to be "quickly" verified. Scott Aaronson underlined the theoretical links between the discussions on computability that led in the 1930s to the discovery of incompleteness and the ongoing debate about *P* and *NP*: The issue of complexity (and "ease" of computation, even if incomplete) prolongs the previous controversy, and, actually, Gödel participated in both debates. Aaronson also suggests that, in a world where $P=NP$, one could "generate Shakespeare's 38th play. For, broadly speaking, that which we can compress we can understand, and that which we can understand we can predict."[1]

Even if there were an algorithmic description (in *NP*) of how to generate a play "by" Shakespeare or a poem "by" Baudelaire, and even if we were to verify or "authenticate" such an apocryphal text (through philologically internal proofs, for instance), it would remain that we would not have discovered the algorithmic path to the emergence of the art the Bard or the *poète maudit* once created. At most, we would *reinvent* a work à la Baudelaire or à la Shakespeare, without ever creating the *possibility* of such oeuvres—without reaching the *poiēsis* of poetry. Mathematical incompleteness and uncomputability appear to be cognitive renditions of the noetic fissures that lead us to the intellective. Roger Penrose insisted on the *nonalgorithmic* side of thinking and linked it to "mathematical insight"—I'd say *creation*. Penrose's ensuing Platonism and his quest for a new quantum physics of the brain are wholly dispensable.

1. Scott Aaronson, "NP-Complete Problems and Physical Reality," 19. http://www.scottaaronson.com/papers/npcomplete.pdf.

tive lyrics could be "compressed," even though the effects (and affects) of saying almost twenty times "Touch me" over the course of one minute accomplish more than the notation of the same words followed by the number of utterances.[19] Similar remarks could be formed on self-commenting words such as TV on the Radio's ad lib "My repetition: my repetition is this."[20] Any description that is shorter than the original will simplify the latter or give us an "output" that masks the "input." This is why the paraphrase of a poem is always sketchy.

2.12.1 Conversely, what makes a poem what it is, with its sounds and rhythms, with its intricate composition and dense allusions, fosters explication. Commentaries are noticeably longer and more explicit than what they are applied to. In exposing the artifice, we tacitly admit that any attempt to "unpack things" will still be incapable of addressing the full specter of interpretations and will lag behind the "economy" of the poem.

2.12.2 Brevity is one way to make sense of the inherent compression of the poetic. [[35]]

2.12.3 Translation makes the severe compression of poetry more palpable. It was certainly logical for hardcore partisans of artificial intelligence from the 1950s onward to posit the automated translation of poems as a benchmark. They failed.

2.12.3.0 "Nothing is translatable, nothing is untranslatable," Derrida rightly wrote.[21] Translation as such (including at least the exact identity of meanings from one language to the other, conservation of prosodic elements and meaningful word order or syntax, transmission of connotations and social usages of speech) is *impossible*. But translation is still *feasible*, and it occurs all the time. Language is opaque, yes, but being also operative and open, it allows some semantic mapping among idioms. Even engines such as Google Translate (abandoning the high ambitions of yesteryear AI and essentially relying on human informants) can provide acceptable versions of mainly referential texts across languages, especially when the latter have historical and/or grammatical commonalities and when they produce large mineable corpora.

The translation of a poem is similarly impossible, while still feasible, and it also occurs all the time. However, many traits of poetry are attached to speech properties that do not map well onto other idioms. The dual lesson of Douglas Hofstadter's *Le Ton Beau de Marot* is that one can in fact translate a French poem of the Renaissance into contemporary American English in many different ways but that no rendition will grasp the entirety (or even the ma-

35. *Poetic brevity in Bashō's "Old Pond" haiku.*

Poetic brevity is often associated with intellectual condensation. This is true with the aphoristic (e.g., the Qohelet), the oracular (e.g., the Delphic corpus), or the fragmented (e.g., what Theodor Adorno called Paul Celan's "infinite discretion").[1] However, some short forms have also been described as being minimally compressed. Roland Barthes, in particular, suggested that the Japanese haiku "is not a rich thought that is reduced [*we would say* 'compressed'] to a brief form."[2] Originally, haiku were supposed to take part in a much longer and collaborative piece of linked poetry. Through an aesthetic decision at some point in the seventeenth century, what once was a unit in a larger ensemble became a standalone piece. It is true that Japanese haiku do not seem to offer much in hermeneutic terms, unless they are being allegorized, which—by the way—happens frequently.

古池や蛙飛び込む水の音
furuike ya ⋮ *kawazu tobikomu* ⋮ *mizu no oto*
•
old pond ⋮ a frog leaps in ⋮ sound of water.[3]

Bashō's "old pond" haiku either is approached as "a brief event that finds its just form at once"[4] and remains rather straightforwardly descriptive or is "translated" into a Buddhist manifesto on impermanence. Whereas the unpacking of semantic content is quite close in length to the text itself, Bashō's haiku compresses different *modes of reading.* The "scene" stays identical; its noetic configuration varies.

In one geometrical approach, the three *on* (or members) of the poem explore three *cuts* within space. The first part delineates an object—the pond—by the insertion of what Japanese poetics call a *cutting word* (here, *ya*); the frog leap delimits a subspace, from the shore to the water; the last *on* focuses on the point of arrival into the water, the depression that is the source of a sound. The progression of the *haiku* is a kind of montage (to follow Eisenstein), with three different close-ups, or a zoom. Another understanding, certainly more "Western," would consider the parts of the poem like a logical chain, as the one found in syllogisms: if *A* (*old pond*) and *B* (*a frog leap*), then *C* (*water sound*). A third framing would be negative, almost Mallarméan. There, the haiku would capture the instant *after* the small animal entered the pond, and only the absence of the frog—as revealed by the plop—would give a hindsight of the scene. Incidentally, this is approximately Barthes's reading. In a fourth perspective, we are dealing with a *tological* description of what is, a minimal evocation of the minimal level of being, akin to what Tristan Garcia, in my view (though not necessarily his), suggests in *Form and Object.* All these modes of reading (as well as others) are contained, and compressed, in the few syllables of the haiku—despite the rather invariant transcript of a "brief event" that, notwithstanding allegory, remains interpretatively poor. This poem does not compact what it is about but its own discursive aboutness.

---

1. Theodor W. Adorno, *Ästhetische Theorie* (Frankfurt: Suhrkamp, 1990), 477; my translation from the German.

2. Roland Barthes, *L'empire des signes* (Genève: Skira, 1980), 98; my translation from the French.

3. Bashō, *Bashō and His Interpreters* (Stanford, Calif.: Stanford University Press, 1991), 140–142; my rendition from the Japanese. There are countless translations of this poem. The very number of frogs is undetermined in the original.

4. Barthes, *L'empire des signes*, 98.

jority) of the effects of the original. Hofstadter was certainly not the first to show this phenomenon, yet he was one of the rare cognitive scientists to emphasize it. A poem's "*untranslatable*" does not derive from its "concepts"; it depends on its own *praxis*. All the problems that one would face with another kind of text are here heightened to a maximum. Translating the poetic practice is barely feasible, for too much volatile and epiphenomenal information is encapsulated in verse. At the same time, with intense attention and effort, a poem's praxis is somehow *transferrable*. The "best" translations combine the ordinary and feasible task of the translator with the extraordinary duty to transfer *poiēsis* into a new verbal artifact. They *allegorize* the original in a new language.

The "poetic" to be transferred is both cognitive and intellective. Images or narrative structures suffer fewer distortions when they are moved across languages, and such relative—very relative—conservation may incidentally explain why blunt universalistic approaches to poetry focus so much on metaphors and comparisons while concurrently investing in (narrative) epos rather than in lyric. Now, translation has an immediate impact on rhythm or alliterations. Transfers will create similar effects, though not always in the same instances and with obviously diverging meanings. If the cognitive is displaced and reconstituted, intellection will differ. Forms and sorts of compression might be partly, though rather successfully, conveyed, even if the density of a specific passage is flattened by its translation. [[36]] [[37]] [[38]]

36. *Poeticity and automated translation in songs by Gérard Manset and Stromae.*

The inner resistance to translation is immediately felt in well-crafted lyrics of popular songs, dissipating the idea that poetic "untranslatables" would be reserved to high-culture artifacts. Gérard Manset, who is certainly the most impressive writer in French rock music, would perfectly illustrate the density of song words. If images are by principle translatable through their tropology, a hyperbolic comparison like "Comme pollen | Dans le grand tumulte des cieux"[1] bypasses its English rendition. Google Translate wishes to emendate the sentence (as many human philologists would unfortunately do) into "As pollen | In the tumult of heaven." This discards the redundancy of "grand tumulte" • "huge tumult," decompressing it as a mere "tumult" (thereby erasing the epithet), while preferring "heaven" to what should rather be "heavens" (*cieux* is a plural in French, with religious or poetic undertones). A less interventionist translation machine, SYSTRAN, suggests a prosaic "Like pollen | In the great tumult of the skies," where the otherwise correct "great" adds unwelcome ambiguity. A more adequate English translation ("As pollen | In the vast tumult of the skies") would still be grammatically incapable of retaining the nonstandard French phrase "comme ⌀ pollen," where the unexpected lack of article or partitive structure is, in fact, poetizing speech. "As pollen" is a definitely accurate, though "lossy," version of the original.

Even in the realm of more straightforward mass culture, Stromae's sung critique of Twitter and Facebook entitled "Carmen," including and playing on American words within Belgian French, is only translatable through the addition of gloss—which largely spoils the pleasure the original creates.

> Prends garde à toi
> Et à tous ceux qui vous like
> Les sourires en plastique sont souvent des coups d'hashtag
> •
> You better beware
> Beware of all those who *like* you
> Plastic smiles often hashtag with an axe[2]

would require to be unpacked in translation, with notes on the use of the English imports "like" and "hashtag," on the puns "coups d'hashtag"/"coups de hache"—and maybe on the quote of Bizet's habanera in the first line.

---

1. Gérard Manset, "Capitaine Courageux," in *Revivre* (EMI France, 1992); my translation from the French.

2. Stromae, "Carmen," in *Racine carrée* (Island Records, 2013); my translation from the French.

37. *The truncation of Edgar Allan Poe's poetics in the French translations of "The Raven" by Charles Baudelaire and Stéphane Mallarmé.*

Poor translations of poetry abound, so let us consider two remarkable renditions, Charles Baudelaire's and Stéphane Mallarmé's versions of Edgar Allan Poe's *The Raven*, in particular its third stanza:

> And the silken sad uncertain rustling of each purple curtain
> Thrilled me—filled me with fantastic terrors never felt before;
> So that now, to still the beating of my heart, I stood repeating
> "'Tis some visitor entreating entrance at my chamber door—
> Some late visitor entreating entrance at my chamber door;—
> This it is and nothing more." (Poe)
>
> •
>
> Et le soyeux, triste et vague bruissement des rideaux pourprés me pénétrait, me remplissait de terreurs fantastiques, inconnues pour moi jusqu'à ce jour ; si bien qu'enfin, pour apaiser le battement de mon cœur, je me dressai, répétant : « C'est quelque visiteur qui sollicite l'entrée à la porte de ma chambre, quelque visiteur attardé sollicitant l'entrée à la porte de ma chambre ;—c'est cela même, et rien de plus. » (Baudelaire)
>
> Et de la soie l'incertain et triste bruissement en chaque rideau purpural me traversait—m'emplissait de fantastiques terreurs pas senties encore : si bien que, pour calmer le battement de mon cœur, je demeurais maintenant à répéter « C'est quelque visiteur qui sollicite l'entrée, à la porte de ma chambre—quelque visiteur qui sollicite l'entrée, à la porte de ma chambre ; c'est cela et rien de plus. » (Mallarmé)[1]

The most visible aspects of regulation are left out in French. The heterometric sixain becomes a paragraph, and rhymes disappear. The loss of the recurring [ɔr] is very significant, since the rhyme throughout the poem prepares the raven's repetition of "nevermore" and "Lenore." What about Poe's unusual recourse to trochaic tetrameters? In deliberately abandoning those aspects of the original, Baudelaire dissolves the metrical into the prose. Mallarmé's paragraphs rely on numerous groups of seven syllables, with some uncertainties in counting given diction and the fate of the "*e muet*." Odd numbers of syllables in French verses have always been scarce (in the same *fin-de-siècle*, Verlaine devotes himself to the exploration of the *vers impair*), so Mallarmé might try to emulate Poe in selecting a rare poetic device. Still, the lack of exact regularity and visibility in his French text does not retain Poe's ostentatious artificiality. Mallarmé, then, unlike Baudelaire, transfers elements of that poetics to the lexical and syntactic levels, with the very rare and archaic form "purpural" • "purpureal" (transposing "purple"), the grammatical anteposition of "de la soie" • "of silk" (instead of "silken" • "soyeux," chosen by Baudelaire), or with the strange "pas senties encore" (an odd syntactic calque of "never felt before"). Poe's metrical baroque may not coincide with the preciosity of speech that Mallarmé elects as a substitute.

Strong elements of repetitions and parallelisms have excellent equivalents in French, like the fourth and fifth lines of the stanza or the initial alliteration in [s] (to "silken sad uncertain rustling" respond "soyeux, triste et vague bruissement" and "soie l'incertain et triste bruissement"). Others are more or less lost, like "Thrilled me—filled me" (the rather banal assonance "me pénétrait, me remplissait" for Baudelaire; the better rhyme "me traversait—m'emplissait" with Mallarmé) and "entreating entrance" (even though one could hear a muffled echo between "visiteur" • "visitor" and "sollicite" • "solicits"). The pun of "some late visitor" is effaced, as the adjective vanishes in Mallarmé's version or is adapted in "attardé" • "tardy" by Baudelaire. Poe's rhythmical inventions are difficult to keep. "So that now, to still the beating of my heart, I stood repeating," for instance, combines an internal rhyme involving the reflexive terms of "beating" and "repeating," the only two words that are not monosyllabic. Mallarmé's rendition "Si bien que, pour calmer le battement de mon cœur, je demeurais maintenant à répéter" is flat, notwithstanding the [m] alliteration that identifies the sentence as a discursive unit. Baudelaire creates a new rhythm in French, based on alternating series of three or four syllables ending with a stress ("si bien qu'en**fin**, pour apaiser le battement de mon **cœur**, je me dressai, répé**tant**"). Such an effect, however, might sound a bit too harmonious and regular, compared with Poe's more chaotic verse. Here and there, gratuitous emendations also simplify the original, as when "et" • "and" is added by both Baudelaire and Mallarmé (respectively: "Et le soyeux, triste et vague bruissement," "Et de la soie l'incertain et triste bruissement"), whereas the English, with comparable rules for the coordination of adjectives, has "And the silken sad ∅ uncertain rustling." All in all, the French renditions compress prosodic, lexical, or metrical aspects in otherwise almost word-by-word translations that also "stay true" to the narrative. In this respect, "Le corbeau," in these two French hypostases, is a poem—not merely a "souvenir" of the original. And still, despite Baudelaire's and Mallarmé's own best efforts, the poetics of "The Raven" is largely truncated by its journey into French.

---

1. Claude Michel Cluny, ed., *Le livre des quatre corbeaux: Poe, Baudelaire, Mallarmé, Pessoa* (Paris: La différence, 1998), 108 (Poe), 117–118 (Baudelaire), 125–126 (Mallarmé).

38. *Tokenism, paraphrase, and translation of Petrarch's initial poem of the* Canzoniere.

Here is the opening sonnet of Petrarch's *Canzoniere*, followed by my admittedly idiosyncratic translation:

Voi ch'ascoltate in rime sparse il suono
Di quei sospiri ond'io nudriva 'l core
In sul mio primo giovenile errore
Quand'era in parte altr'uom da quel ch'i' sono,
Del vario stile in ch'io piango et ragiono
Fra le vane speranze, e 'l van dolore
Ove sia chi per prova intenda amore
Spero trovar pietà—non che perdono.
Ma ben veggio or sì come al popol tutto
Favola fui gran tempo—onde sovente
Di me medesmo meco mi vergogno.
Et del mio vaneggiar vergogna è 'l frutto
E 'l pentersi, e 'l conoscer chiaramente
Che quanto piace al mondo è breve sogno.

•

You who're listening through disparate rhymes to the sound
Of those sighs with which I nourished the heart
In the error of my first youth
As I was partly other than the man I am,
Of the varied style I use for crying and arguing
Amidst the vain hopes, and vain pain
Where stand those who by proof know love,
I hope to find pity—if not mercy.
But now I see well how all the people
Made for a long time a fable of me—whence often
By myself I am ashamed of myself.
And of my vanities shame is the fruit
And repenting, and clearly grasping
That all which pleases in the world is a brief dream.[1]

More than twenty different English translations of Petrarch's sonnet, ranging from the late eighteenth century to the present, could be gathered. They are widely divergent. The anacolutha of the first two quatrains pose great interpretive difficulties. The other peculiarities of the poem's syntax and diction are leveled down. The reflexive terms selected by Petrarch (*rhymes, sound, style, arguing*) are often discarded, for fear of diminishing the alleged—and here fallacious—naiveté of medieval poetry. The echoes and rhymes between "sono" • "sound," "sono" • "am," and "sogno" • "dream" are often silenced. The list could go on. Nonetheless, an automated latent semantic analysis yields results establishing some strong cosine similarity across most translations. In more lay terms, the English texts are semantically and literarily diverse, but, objectively and quantitatively, they "look alike" and may sometimes offer strong resemblance. By "overlapping" those English versions of the original sonnet, one could even isolate a "core message" that is frequently kept by the translators, though often with different words. The "common denominator" of most standard English translations could read like this:

> *You who hear in rhymes the sound of my sighs on which I fed my heart in my youthful error, when I was in part another; having varied ways of sobbing amid vain hopes and sorrow, in anyone who loved I hope to find pardon or pity. But I see now that I was ridiculed by many, and I am ashamed. Shame is the fruit, as are repentance and knowing that joy in the world is a dream.*

This "token poem" is not wholly unlike "Voi ch'ascoltate . . ." Some critics might argue that this is exactly what the actual poem is about—or even *is*. This would reduce a literary piece to its paraphrase and most of its compressed information to superfluous ornamentation or mnemonic aid. Bad philology did not wait for the era of artificial intelligence to oversimplify poetic density, as a glance at the paraphrases in some Renaissance editions of Petrarch would show. We face an epistemological, political, and ethical issue: Should we promote, teach, comment, write, and read *token poems* rather than poems, in the name of communicational transparency, of democratization, of the current limits of computers, of the people who are hooked to them? My answer is not a sigh; it is a resounding *no*. In poetry, no tokenism, please.

---

1. Petrarch, *Canzoniere*, poem 1; my translation from the Italian. I am basically adopting the Italian text given in Giuseppe Savoca's edition of Petrarch, *Rerum vulgarium fragmenta* (Florence, Italy: Olschki, 2008), 3, though correcting (and adapting) the punctuation on the basis of the Vatican manuscript, whose diplomatic transcription by Ettore Modigliani will be found in Petrarch, *Rervm vulgarivm fragmenta* (Rome: Società filologica romana, 1904), 17.

2.12.4 The hermetic can only haunt poetry.

2.12.4.0 Hermetic poetry is not sealed off. Quite the opposite, it is indispensably, extremely, *open* to interpretation. "Code cracking" is a self-denying hermeneutics, aiming to compress the incompressible. Obfuscated poetry is a parody of the hermetic; it is a delusional cryptology.

2.13 *Poetry incorporates cognitive dissonance and draws on nonconsistent logical reasoning.*

2.13.0 Cognitive dissonance, or any strong impression of impossibility in the face of what a poem is stating, is induced by the performative disposition of a complex verbal artifact. The movement of deautomation through reautomation only adds to this, as does the status of fictional literary objects. Incompatibilities, contradictions, tensions are otherwise transformed into *notions* that many individual poems work through. Intellective contradictions or incompossibilities are neither "explosive" nor "trivial"; they are more than just vague. They are *transconsistent* beyond what even the symbols of nonstandard formalized logics are apt to point at. Poetic contradictions are not always lies, licenses, errors, or episodes of senselessness; they are becoming *significant*, as we think and embody them. [[39]]

2.13.1 In poems, logical obstacles become significations. [[40]]

2.14 *Poetry is aptly recursive and reflexive.*

2.14.0 For being a catchword in debates about human and animal cognition, "recursion" is a rather proliferating and multivalent concept. If we recognize in recursion the need for *multiple layers*, some level of *self-similarity*, and the drive toward *further replications* of the current structure, then we see that the metatextuality of literary theory is a recursive process. Poems that comment on themselves; draw attention to their artificiality; include references to writing, speaking, and reading; or summon characters that versify, sing, or talk can be found in the traditions of all continents, across millennia. Texts are embedded within themselves and the depiction of their creation or reception. A sentiment for artistic achievement is a consequence of the cognitive disorientation we go through and of the intellective challenge we encounter. [[41]]

2.14.1 Reflexivity, in the arts, is a particular brand of recursion, relying on self-presentation. Or: there is no *art* without self-presentation.

2.14.1.0 The *art* of poetry is its reflexive image.

2.14.1.1 Poetic reflexivity is figurative.

39. *Oxymora and contradictions in Louise Labé's "I live, I die . . ."*

European love poetry is particularly prone to express contradictions in the symptomatology of feelings. In the Renaissance, Petrarchism popularized the topos again. A beautiful example is to be found in Louise Labé's sonnet "I live, I die . . ." • "Ie vis, ie meurs . . . ,"[1] where the lyrical subject lists her exposure to opposite (and extreme) conditions, such as "I am burning & drowning" • "ie me brule & me noye" or "Of a sudden I laugh & weep" • "Tout à un coup ie ris & ie larmoye." The beginning of the sestet ("Ainsi Amour inconstamment me meine" • "And so Love drives me inconstant") could be read, with today's positive knowledge, as an apt description of conflicting emotions in the central nervous system, when the sub- and neocortical dimensions of sentiments use nonconcurring pathways. Psychoanalysis would also posit an instantiation of the subject as id, ego, and superego. A poem, nevertheless, is more than descriptive. However accurate Labé's depiction of love could be from the (para)scientific viewpoint, its noetic matrix is contradictions, impossibilities, oxymora. Before *explaining* the latter as the inevitable effects of love (a position transiently assumed by the text itself), we have to handle the power of the contradictions in terms. Labé skillfully varies the logical juncture between the opposite, through simple juxtaposition or coordination. Familiar concepts might sustain those tensions—there is, after all, an old tradition of lyric dialogue between Heart and Reason. In this regard, one could still diminish the scandal of assertions like "I live, I die" by casting them as illusions or beliefs. Textual resistance remains nevertheless, for one usually admits in doxastic logic that

$$B(p)\wedge B(q)\Leftrightarrow B(p\wedge q).$$

So we'd still end up with some violation of the standard principle of noncontradiction. The emotional dynamics the sonnet finally suggests (a "cyclothymic" effect, if I may say so) is at odds with at least the first part of the text. If "sudden" changes are marked, they are always expressed in the present tense, for example: "All of a sudden I dry & I bloom" • "Tout en un coup ie seiche & ie verdoye." It is as if the text itself were marked by a systematic inconsistence. One sentence introduces a strong ambiguity on both thought (or thinking) and its object: "And when I think to have most pain, | Without thinking of it I find myself out of harm's way" • "Et quand ie pense auoir plus de douleur, | Sans y penser ie me treuue hors de peine." The *it* • *y* is to be determined. "Sans y penser" is idiomatic French for "without thinking," but an object *y* is expressed, which has even more importance in the dialect of Lyons, where "*y*" possesses a grammatically broader function than it does in Paris. In the line "And so Love drives me inconstant," the original adverb "inconstamment" would normally refer to Love, which sounds wrong, given Cupid's stubborn plan to confuse the *I*. In both cases, some logical disturbance contaminates the very poetics of the text.

1. Louise Labé, *Sonnets*, poem 7 ("Ie vis, ie meurs . . .") for all quotes; my translation from the French. I am keeping the spelling of the original edition, *Euvres* (Lyon: Tournes, 1556).

2.14.1.1.0 Figuring, within a poem, the act of reading, singing, writing, composing, commenting, or reciting is specular. Turning poets into characters plays the same function.

2.14.1.1.1 A *mise en abyme* requires an even higher level of self-similarity, with a reflexive focus on the agent and the content of speech.

2.14.1.1.2 Allegorization pertains to recursive modes of reading and writing. Allegory does not have to be taken as the arch-category of literary reflexivity.

2.14.1.1.3 Figurative reflexivity is potentially produced by other arts, such as cinema, comics, sculpture, or painting.

2.14.1.2 Poetic reflexivity is discursive.

2.14.1.2.0 In the maximal semantics of a literary work, markers of metadiscourse are not neutral. They point the way toward the verbal reality of the oeuvre. Foreign languages, divergent idiomatic registers, heterogeneous expressions or words also become self-referential indexes. Invocations to the Muse or the readers go one step beyond. The genre of *ars poetica* is wholly reflexive—as practiced by Horace and Nicolas Boileau or by Lu Ji in his "*Fu* on literature" (文賦).

2.14.1.2.1 Performative adherence draws attention to structural replications. Iconic effects of rhythm, calligraphy, or enjambments and *rejets* belong to those, as do self-descriptive structures or sentences commenting upon themselves through their utterance (as when Hamlet's "The rest is silence" is followed with silence).

2.14.1.2.2 Performative contradictions, from preteritions to more robust *adunata*, offer self-similarity through position and negation.

40. *The affirmation of contradictions in Charles Baudelaire's* "Heautontimoroumenos."

What happens when I read the following lines by Charles Baudelaire?

Je suis la plaie et le couteau!
Je suis le soufflet et la joue!
Je suis les membres et la roue,
Et la victime et le bourreau!

•

I am the wound and the dagger!
I am the blow and the cheek!
I am the members and the wheel,
Both the victim and the executioner![1]

The intellection that we share through the reading of Baudelaire's poem on (and thanks to) the external margins of rational protocols proceeds through a *cumulative*, *dynamic*, and *assertive* gesture. As such, its formula (if we needed one) would be:

$$\vdash(\alpha\wedge\neg\alpha\wedge\beta) \qquad \exists\alpha, \exists\beta.$$

We could imagine that we have found an equation for literary thinking *in general*, or (rather) for the cognitive trace of what lies ahead of mental computation. It allows us to go farther than what the mathematician Newton Da Costa names the paraconsistent assertion of both $\alpha\wedge\neg\alpha$. The right tack $\vdash$ (with its stroke on the left) refers to a distinction introduced by Gottlob Frege some twenty years after the first edition of *Les fleurs du Mal*, as he invented modern propositional calculus in his *Begriffsschrift*. Almost nobody really understood the use (in formalized logic) of a distinction between the tack and a simple dash, that is, between the *yes* that is inherent to an "affirmation" of "judgment" (Frege writes *Bejahung* and *Urtheil*) and "a simple link between representations."[2] Wittgenstein even states that the sign is "quite meaningless, logically."[3] I am recuperating this difference to mark the fact that literary signification is not only uttered, not only contemplated, not already written, not automatically computed, not reproduced by an obedient mind, not attended to by some spectator—but also performed by the *I* that ties itself to the transform of the text, the *I* wearing the mask then becoming the very one *I* that is one *and* the other *and* another other. Such an affirmation might well indeed be "quite meaningful, poetically."

---

1. Charles Baudelaire, *Les fleurs du Mal*, poem 73 (1861 ed.); my translation from the French. I worked on this text in *The Intellective Space* (Minneapolis: University of Minnesota Press, 2015), §52.

2. Gottlob Frege, *Begriffschrift*, § I.2; my translation from the German.

3. Ludwig Wittgenstein, *Tractatus Logico-Philosophicus*, §4.442; my translation from the German.

41. *Different types of recursion.*

Within contemporary cognitive studies, *recursion* (whose definition is assuredly more mobile and vague than one would expect from a scientific project)[1] is used to emphasize one of its main aspects or attributes. There is first an emphasis on *infinity*. Recursive structures are possibly endless and are open to very high numbers of reduplications. This might be somewhat true of a mathematical algorithm as such, but it is dubious that any animal mind (including a human one) would actually be able to grasp those *in*finite processes. As for language, *pace* Noam Chomsky, it rarely offers anything that would resemble actually infinite embedding structures. In fact, when facing such motifs, we tend to simplify the architecture and to process elements "in line" instead of *maintaining* the hierarchy among all levels.

Recursion is also used to emphasize mental *embedding*, as established by the line of research on orders of intentionality. Statements of the kind "Cred'ïo ch'ei credette ch'io credesse | che. . ." • "I believe that he believed that I believed | that. . .," to quote Dante's *Inferno*,[2] are common in speech and literature. Here too, there are strict limits to what we can actually envision. Generating and processing orders of intentionality might also differ, with some tendency to ease understanding by mapping recursion onto the last structural iteration.

Finally, recursion may create valid cognitive structures that are almost impossible to decide. Douglas Hofstadter rightly saw the potential for *strange loops*, as well as their numerous occurrences in the arts. Concurrently, literary theory and criticism are filled with such loops (under other names).

---

1. For an overview, see Maurício Dias Martins, "Distinctive Signatures of Recursion," *Philosophical Transactions of the Royal Society B* 367 (2012): 2055–2064.
2. Dante, *Inferno*, canto XIII, lines 25–26; my translation from the Italian.

2.14.1.2.3 Discursive reflexivity has an equivalent in nonverbal structures, through the self-presentation of the visual, the musical phrase, or dance movements.

2.14.2 Poetic reflexivity often displays a concatenation of means. [[42]]

2.14.3 Through poetic recursion, our minds are brought onto the outside limits of what they commonly fathom.

2.14.3.0 Performative contradictions affecting reading and writing catch us off guard. [[43]]

42. *Levels of reflexivity in Dante's first canto of the* Inferno.

Dante's *Commedia* serves a political, moral, and theological purpose that is the outcome of its initial self-presentation. The first canto of the *Inferno* introduces Dante as a first-person narrator and character being guided by the poet Virgil. Such figuration is enlarged up to *mise en abyme*, as soon as the *I* understands who he is talking to and states that Virgil is "of the other poets both honor and light" • "de li altri poeti onore e lume."[1] More than this, the *I* says to his interlocutor, "You are my master and my author" • "Tu se' lo mio maestro e'l mio autore,"[2] ceding the authorship of himself (as an author) to his illustrious predecessor. Allegorization is constantly proposed, from the very first line ("Nel mezzo del cammin di nostra vita"[3]), where "the path of our life" is also the very path that narratively leads the *I* to the gates of Hell, or to the encounter with both the beast and the ideal poet. Discursive reflexivity is further enacted through metadiscourse, encompassing Latin words, when Virgil tells who he is in the form of a riddle: "Nacqui *sub Iulio*" • "I was born *sub Iulio*."[4] The *terza rima* Dante invented (with interlinked tercets based on the recursive rhyme schema ABA BCB CDC . . .) accrues to overall reflexivity through poetic technique. The thousands of echoing tercets almost mirror the spiraled and concentric shapes of Heaven, Purgatory, and Hell that Gustave Doré brilliantly rendered in his engravings for the *Commedia*. Such a sophisticated recursion, pervading so many levels of a very long and rich oeuvre, its specular—and spectacular—*effet d'ensemble* identify the *apt art* of poetry.

---

1. Dante, *Inferno*, canto I, line 82.
2. Ibid., canto I, line 85.
3. Ibid., canto I, line 1.
4. Ibid., canto I, line 70.

2.14.4 We wander as we contemplate the becoming of ourselves in complex embedding. Doing as if we were not part of what we read diminishes textual capabilities and incapacitates *us*, preventing our minds from crossing the line of the (un)thinkable. Gradually, by immersing ourselves into a verbally recursive artifact, by applying textual logic one step further, we tend to feel the boundaries of our thought process—as well as the urge to continue and perform the promise of the poem. [[44]]

2.14.5 The poetic aptitude for multiplied recursion is enmeshed with an odd performative cohesion (not exactly coherent, not always con-

43. *Impossible writing, impossible reading in Antonin Artaud's late work.*

In the last years of his life, Antonin Artaud wrote almost constantly, producing vast amounts of text that radically defies interpretation.[1] Not only does he often repudiate reality and its inhabitants as being a gigantic trick against himself, not only does he deny that he has a mind, but he incessantly refurbishes his language, attributing both unpredictable and volatile meanings to many words he uses (even in the course of the same stanza) and coining vocables. In one of his notebooks, Artaud indicates à propos his glossolalia: "The secret of this language is that it can mean 100 contradictory things" • "Le secret de ce langage est qu'il veut dire 100 choses contradictoires."[2] More globally, "words *mean* nothing" • "les mots ne veulent rien dire."[3] Artaud is also explicit about his writings: They are impossible to write and impossible to read. He claims that *Suppôts et suppliciations* (the last volume he prepared for publication) is the

> type of a fucking boring book that is absolutely impossible to read,
> that nobody ever read through and through,
> not even its author
> •
> type du livre emmerdant absolument impossible à lire,
> que personne n'a jamais lu de bout en bout,
> même pas son auteur.[4]

Concurrently, his quest is for "an impossible writing" • "un impossible écrit."[5] All of this, nevertheless, has been written and read, at least in some sense. Following Artaud until the end is a dangerous task, and some of his admirers and companions (like Colette Thomas or Jacques Prevel) certainly lost themselves in the process. For any of us, the only way to read this corpus as it purports to be read is by *nonreading* it and by considering it to be only a living thing (and not a text that is alive in us). Since this is not tenable, we are doomed to fail, and this programmed fiasco has been, for decades, the source of mechanical and reductive interpretations of Artaud. Unless, of course, this failure is also the writer's, who might have thereby chosen a sublime sacrifice, where the lack of success according to its claimed ambition would still be an apotropaic demonstration of genius. Artaud's final endeavor offers singular variations on double-bind sentences ("do not read this!", "the sentence you are reading is not written") that *put us to the test*. If I am willing to be challenged in everything I believe in and in the very act of being, my mind is creating signification through the debacle of meaning and thought. This new thinking lives with me.

1. Here, I am drawing on my first book, *De l'attrait à la possession* (Paris: Hermann, 2005), 197–225.

2. Antonin Artaud, *Œuvres complètes* (Paris: Gallimard, 1956–1994), 24:270; see 25:16; my translation from the French.

3. Ibid., 23:140.

4. Ibid., 14-2:234.

5. Ibid., 23:79.

sistent) in which we partake. We are living proof that the untenable has its locus—us.

2.15 *Poetry creates detachable, movable, and livable significations for psychological selves.*

2.15.0 In the archeology of the self are bodily proprioception and the right cognitive infrastructure—including cortical architecture and some "extended" apparatus, like the mirror that precipitates self-recognition in individuals of a few animal species. To extendedness belong many traits of symbolic culture and speech that bootstrap and consolidate the self, from portraits to the middle voice in grammar. The self is not the *I* but a looped relation to the latter. The self proceeds from bifurcation. This leads to structural abstraction (reflexivity) and to further personal self-bifurcation (with all the many instances that are me: my heart, my body, my soul, my mind, . . .). Personality traits and memories—none of them being the exclusive province of humankind—make me; as such, they are neither my self nor myself. I may be "me" when I reaffirm what I have previously done or felt ("it's me," "it's not me"). I am *I* in what I say (I am). But I always *become* myself in posing the *I* and its relationship to me. Both the *I* and the link to it are susceptible to those variations.

2.15.1 Poetry is offering other ideas, other emotions, and other selves to us.

2.15.1.0 The poetic doubt on the reflexive identity of the I-me enlarges my self beyond myself. [[45]]

2.15.2 So many poems are known by heart that they live with, in, among us. Pieces of poems get detached and rearranged. They give ideas to ponder and words to chew. They enter our memory; they are our

44. *Echoing echoes in Ovid's* Metamorphoses *(III, 357–390).*

In the third book of his *Metamorphoses*, Ovid conjures up the nymph Echo and her unrequited love for Narcissus. Echo cannot directly express her longing for the adolescent; she is only able to repeat the last part of what he says. Ovid uses direct speech three times to describe the interlocution, which makes him redouble his own words in his turn:

dixerat: "ecquis adest?" et "adest" responderat Echo . . .
"huc coeamus" ait . . . "coeamus" rettulit Echo . . .
. . . ait "emoriar, quam sit tibi copia nostri"
rettulit illa nihil nisi "sit tibi copia nostri!"
•
he told: "anyone here?" and Echo responded "here" . . .
"over there! come!" he said . . . "come!" Echo replied . . .
. . . he said "I'll die before I give myself to you"
she could reply nothing but "I give myself to you."[1]

In duplicating the same words in his verses, the writer is obviously *echoing Echo echoing Narcissus*. In the later poetry of the European Renaissance, echoing became a quite popular technique. Echoes are maximal rhymes, making use of semantic inflections. Ovid already plays on meanings: "huc coeamus" • lit. "let us come there together" is an even more explicit allusion to Echo's desires (the verb *coire* also means *to have sex*), while coding the name of the nymph (*coeamus/ Echo*). Echoes are not only found in quotes; they also occur in the narrative itself, through redundancy and paronomasia: "'Quid' inquit" • "'why?' he asked,"[2] "Vocat illa vocantem" • "she calls the one calling"[3] and "ille fugit fugiensque" • "he fled the one fleeing"[4] are not uttered by the nymph or by Narcissus. Those internal repetitions parallel, at another discursive level, the circulation of words in the scene. Such performative adherence contributes to establishing *a poetics aiming to echo the quotations that echo Echo echoing Narcissus.*

This is not Ovid's invention exactly. The *Greek Anthology* collects a few poems dedicated to Echo (or to a statue representing her). One text, by a named Garaudas, is difficult to date, but it only relies on echoes of the last words.[5] An epigram written by Parmenion, who might have been contemporary with Ovid, invokes the "talkative Echo" • "lálon Ēchṓ" to introduce an *I* saying to a *you*: "the speech you speak, I'll return it to you, and if you are silent, | I'll be silent" • "eis sè gàr hòn sù légeis strépsō lógon ḕn dè siōpậs, | sigḗsō."[6] In all likelihood, *echolalia* had been turned into a poetic genre by the ancient Greeks.[7] *The Metamorphoses* would then develop *a poetics echoing a genre that echoes the echoes of Echo echoing the voice of mortals.*

More decisively, Euripides created in 412 BCE a (now lost) tragedy entitled *Andromeda*, which, by the way, Ovid apparently used for his own retelling of that other myth. In one striking episode of the play, Euripides's Andromeda, who has been chained to a rock, only exchanges words with Echo, almost certainly reduced to a voice offstage, repeating the end of the princess's sentences. As early as 411 BCE, Aristophanes recreated the setting with Euripides (now as a character) quoting himself, then echoing, rather hilariously, what was being uttered on the *skēnē*.[8] Ovid, who composes a rhapsodic and encyclopedic work on mutations, could only quote such comic echoes of Echo's tragic echoes. To put it differently, *Ovid, in his reflexive echoes to Echo's echoes, also echoes the genre of poetic echolalia that echoed (or was echoed by) a comedy echoing a tragedy echoing the echoes of the nymph.*

This is where the reader realizes that, by *voicing* the text of *The Metamorphoses*, she also echoes it—and adds another concentric circle. My gloss, quoting echoes of echoes of echoes again, provides additional self-replication. Through criticism, *I am now echoing my embodiment of Ovid's recursive echoes to Echo's echoes, those in echo to the genre of echolalia that may have echoed Aristophanes's "Euripides" echoing the echoes Euripides wrote of Echo's echoes.* As a *voice*, I am becoming an effect of poetic reflexivity. This puzzles me, but this is what I try to compute, or figure out.

---

1. Ovid, *Metamorphoses*, book III, lines 380, 386–387, 391–392; my translation from the Latin.
2. Ibid., book III, line 384.
3. Ibid., book III, line 382; "voce" appears earlier on the same line.
4. Ibid., book III, line 390.
5. *Greek Anthology*, book 16, poem 152.
6. Ibid., book 9, poem 27; my translation from the Greek.
7. See also Tom Philipps, *Pindar's Library: Performance Library and Material Texts* (Oxford: Oxford University Press, 2016), 211–236.
8. Aristophanes, *Thesmophoriazusae*, lines 1070–1080.

memories, both image and caption. As much as mnemonic fixation is eased by poetic repetition, rhythm, and musicality,[22] poems exploit cognitive patterning to insert themselves *within* our memory. We do not only reminisce about the past joy we encountered in hearing or reading a text—we may also *know* this song and that stanza. We sometimes neutralize their force by habituating ourselves, until, one day, we hear them chanting anew. This stands in contrast with many other verbal or visual arts, whose oeuvres (novels, movies, sculptures, video clips, paintings, . . .) cannot be

45. *The I and the personae of poetry.*

From Walt Whitman's "I contain multitudes" in "The Song of Myself"[1] to Rimbaud's "I is another" • "Je est un autre,"[2] or from Borges's "I am the other" • "soy el otro"[3] to Gertrude Stein's "I am I because my little dog knows me,"[4] modern poetry has been tasked with exploring the conundrums of the first person. If Western authors from the last two centuries appear to be warier of this problem, I am not sure they're more *aware* of it than their precursors once were. In one of his songs, Bernart de Ventardorn, the Occitan troubadour, wrote "I never had power over me" • "Anc non agui de me poder," from the day "she let me gaze in her eyes | in a mirror that pleases me much" • "que'm laisset en sos olhs vezer | en un miralh que mout me plai."[5] Sappho, in a poem only recently rediscovered, figures *herself* writing to a *you* that *she* (or *he*) should tell *her* to go ask *the goddess* for *her brother* Charaxos to return safely to port:

> . . . sè d'ou khrē̂
>   taûta noeîsthai, ¶
> allà kaì pémpēn éme kaì kélesthai
> pólla líssesthai basílēan Ḗran
> exíkesthai tuíde sáan ágonta
>   nâa Kháraxon
>
> •
>
> . . . and you should not
>   think about this, ¶
> but rather send me, urging me
> to pray and pray the queen Hera that
> Charaxos would come back home,
>   steering his ship.[6]

The epistle creates multiple—virtual—personae. In this message addressed to a *you*, the *I* is becoming an envoy ("pémpēn éme" • "to send me") that is being told by another person (a person she ventriloquizes) what she will beg Hera to give to her (or Sappho's) brother. This exhortative fiction is diffracting each self. The syntax of the stanza conveys the same idea, with a succession of infinitive forms (five verbs out of six) that are semantically coordinated though grammatically juxtaposed, the attenuation of the expressed subject (an *I* that is uttered just once in one stanza), and the acrobatic disposition of word units at the closing of the quatrain (following the unusual order: "[come back home] [his] [steering] [ship] [Charaxos]"). Identities bifurcate and disseminate; non-coincidence is maintained.

Poetry to be read aloud, improvised, said by an actor on stage, sung, or recited, that is, most poetry, implies *bifurcation* between the biographical author and her text, between textual *deixis* and the voice and body of the performer, between a lead singer and a chorus repeating the same words, between the Muse and the *aoidos*. Both internal and external instances of the *I* accumulate; the *me* gets displaced by the existence of those other *I*; in relating myself to those *persons* and recognizing myself in the portraits of those that are not me, the myself of myself is transformed. Epic, narrative, even didactic poems are far from being exempt from those considerations (through the evocation of textual transmission or calls to sacred inspiration). The lyric is undoubtedly in closer correspondence with Gottfried Benn's sentence "Ein Gedicht ist immer eine Frage nach dem Ich" • "a poem is always a question toward the I."[7] Our selves being shaped by discourse; we are altered when we accept in us those words that could be ours and that de facto are and are not ours. To what extent are we altered? Is it for long? This is difficult to say. Yet, I contend that the *personae* of poetry—their necessary expression, their operative defection—equip me for thinking that: (a) I may be more than myself, (b) I may be more than the nonself of the self that I have, (c) that our selves may be other than themselves. Like my early experience of self-recognition that made me grasp that I was the child in the mirror, poetic thinking brings me forward and suggests that what I become I am not—even though I may be (something like) me. Any "identity politics" is revealed by the poetic process of personification to be at best a subsidiary need and at worst an abysmal stupidity. While social rules and the human psyche require the relative stability of the *me*, the shifting *I* of *deixis* as well as our bifurcating selves also *move* us further toward an intellective understanding of "my own" "mind" and "soul." Poetry has shown all this for millennia. After the "mirror stage" is a "poem stage" that our psychogenesis could reach.

---

1. Walt Whitman, stanza 51 of "The Song of Myself," in *Leaves of Grass*.

2. Rimbaud, *Œuvre-vie*, 187; my translation from the French.

3. Jose Luis Borges, "Poema de los dones," in *Obra Poética* (Buenos Aires: Emecé, 1977), 114; my translation from the Spanish.

4. Gertrude Stein, "Identity A Poem" in *A Stein Reader*, ed. Ulla Dydo (Evanston, Ill.: Northwestern University Press, 1993), 593.

5. Bernart de Ventadorn, *Lieder* (Halle: Niemeyer, 1915), 251, "Can vei la lauzeta mover" (poem 40), lines 17, 19–20; my translation from the Occitan.

6. Sappho, "Brothers poem," lines 3–8. I am reproducing (with one minor emendation) the text of the papyrus edited by Dirk Obbink, "Two New Poems by Sappho," *Zeitschrift für Papyrologie und Epigraphik* 189 (2014): 37; my translation from the Greek.

7. Gottfried Benn, *Sämtliche Werke* (Stuttgart: Klett-Cotta, 1986–2003), 6:4; my translation from the German.

both accurately remembered and reproduced by a human agent (except perhaps by an idiot savant or a master forger). Beside the theoretical teachings of the "poem stage," lyrics and verses populate our selves.

2.15.2.0 The poetic fragments or works we take "with us" are elements we can recite—and partly relive. Not that we automatically perceive with vivid colors the scene or image that is depicted in a quatrain as if it were recollections of notable moments of our existence. But, through recitation and right after it, we may access a dual range of emotions (the affect *in* the line, the affect *of* the line) that we remember having felt before. The repetition that rote learning favors, *if* it is semantic and not only "autonoetic," implies that each of us may be confronted many times with such relived sentiments. This self-relation to our own emotions through empathy and memory blurs the line of what *I* once felt. The affective core, conjoined with reiteration, draws poems closer to autobiographical memory—or to the mental consolidation that dreams allow. The verses we know *implant* in us memories of affects and passions that we can recognize as being ours, as parts of our life history—even if they have been in fact delivered to us by verbal artifacts. The way *I* love or scorn is also built on the subjective integration of affects that my mind considers to have been, and still be, "my own." This is not propaganda, where "a lie" is *known* to be "a truth." This is mental alteration and enlargement through remembrance. Hence, reidentification (of what was "mine" and what was not) is pointless, since I changed myself to accommodate the past brought up by the new recollection.

Such an enlargement is sometimes responsible for actual changes in the emotional registry of an entire milieu, from where behaviors reach a critical mass and percolate, finding broader relays in the collective ordering of imaginaries. Romantic poetry—disseminated through lyrics, rote learning, the practice of keepsakes, and individual rereading—decisively contributed to an appreciation of nature and to changes in social norms regarding death or love. Through sung and recited poetry, the Harlem Renaissance and *négritude* movements instilled the conditions for a political attitude made of indignation and pride that served the purpose of desegregation and decolonization. In the *longue du-*

rée, the political acceptance and promotion of poetry is also intertwined with the hope that *oeuvres* would durably contribute to some socially sanctioned psychogenesis.

That bits of poems could come back to us by passing the threshold of consciousness, that we can recite them without even "thinking" or while suddenly understanding them afresh, or that repetitive verbal forms could be repeated again and again puts poetry close to *rumination*. Being full with words, and being as if animated by them in a state of limited consciousness, assimilates the poetic experience with the feelings of elation and disorientation associated with altered states of mind, like inebriation or even ecstasy (for the writer especially). The iterative and mnemonic aspects of poetry reinforce such psychological dispositions, with an added element of "self-control."

2.15.3 A profound misconception of literature confines it to the domain of emotions, percepts, or "aesthetics" (this latter word being an unfortunate invention of the Enlightenment era, programmatically limiting the artistic experience to the senses). Poetry creates emotions in us, and it shapes our selves—but it is absurd to claim that it is only, or even *essentially*, affective and subjective. "Movable significations" are not autonomously produced by a sacred idiom that would speak to us. The reality of language is not being superseded or effaced by the discourse of a poem; it is being challenged. The tensions or potential contradictions that stem from the poetic and communicational usages of words stun, amaze, bewilder us—and make us receptive to others' way of feeling *and* thinking. The clear-cut separation of the noetic and the affective is theoretically unsound and neurologically undefendable. [[46]]

2.15.4 And in brief, it is both the contours and content of myself that poems affect. [[47]]

2.16 Imagery, regulations, musicality, rhythm or transconsistence are what poetry thinks with. *Notions* and *topoi* are what poetry thinks through.

2.16.0 Poetry is not thematically bounded. From a transcultural and transhistorical perspective, poems can deal with everything: the combat of rats and frogs, pubic hair, the praise of dead heroes, or

46. *Evocation and self-imprinting in Émile Benveniste's* Baudelaire *and beyond.*

In the hundreds of notes he assembled for an article on Baudelaire that he would never write, Émile Benveniste sadly reduces poetry to the emotional. But he also makes a series of propositions that we could reemploy and subvert. In trying to show that a word in a text by Baudelaire does not function as in "ordinary language," Benveniste revisits Saussurean distinctions, positing that a *poetic sign* (or "*symbol*," or "*eicasm*") would have no *referent* but an "*idea of sentiment*" or "*pathēma*" (something felt, as an imprint) and that it would offer two aspects: the *evoked* (instead of the *signified*) and the *evoker* (rather than the *signifier*). The *evoker* includes the dimensions of rhythms, rhymes, phonological recurrences, and so on. For Benveniste, the mental processing of the *evoked* and the *evoker* creates in the reader an emotional *impression* that is individually constructed and echoes the initial sentiment that drove the writer to compose.[1] If, against the ideas of the linguist, we maintain that the same sign is read extra-ordinarily because it is concurrently and defectively approached in an "ordinary way," we can describe another dynamics. Signification arises from the lack and excess of meaning that prompts me to create where I just parsed. There, my mind performs it as an impression, "filling in" the evoked and imprinting it on my self.

1. I base my reconstruction of Émile Benveniste's hypothesis on his *Baudelaire* (Limoges: Lambert-Lucas, 2011), 138, 398, 410, 558, 582, 586, 588. Note that, for Benveniste, a group of signs is a sign. Benveniste reuses, in a different perspective, Aristotle's conception as laid out in his *On Interpretation*, 16a.

the American supermarket. Within a given tradition, however (it does not need to be linear), one often observes limits to what is sayable. Those boundaries sometimes form a third level of regulation, although they are usually tied to discursive (sub)genres and are more provincial in nature. Such rules are also more diverse and unevenly implemented than are linguistic reorganizations and iterative systems.

2.16.1 "Elevated language" might depend on considerations about the permissible distribution of speech, as well as censorship, in the society at large. Poetic exclusion of words or topics could simply reflect a consensus or a law. Other ways of framing what is said could more indirectly transcribe a social need for firm rules, whatever they are. In seventeenth-century France and Japan—two contemporary

47. *The poem stage in Constantine Cavafy's "The City."*

In one of his early poems ("The City"), Constantine Cavafy begins with: "You said: 'I shall go to another land, I shall go to another sea'" • "Eîpes: 'Thà págō s' állē gê, thà pagō s' állē thálassa.'" *You* and *I*, the *you* that says *I*, the *you* that may well be the *I* of the text in an inner dialogue, are all masks for ourselves. Then, the *you* not only says *I*, with all the necessary marks of *deixis*; he also decomposes himself as a series of properties that, according to the syntax of modern Greek, are insistently said to be "mine": "each endeavor mine" • "prospátheia mou," "the heart mine" • "ē kardiá mou," "the mind mine" • "ho noûs mou," "the gaze mine" • "tò máti mou," "the life mine" • "tēs zoês mou." The final revelation brought by the *I* of the text is that there is no *other*—land, sea, city—for the *I* that is *you*:

> Kainoúrious tópous dèn thà breîs, dèn thá breis álles thálasses . . .
> Pánta stḕn póli autē thà phtháneis. Già tà alloû—mḕ elpízeis—
> dèn ékhei ploîo già sé, dèn ékhei hodó.
> •
> New places won't be found by you, you will not find other seas . . .
> You'll always end up in this very city. As for the rest—abandon your hopes—,
> there is no ship for you, there is no path.[1]

As for me, saying all this again, I am no longer the same old me; I am moving my self through the other other's gaze. Beyond the poem stage, I am intellectively different.

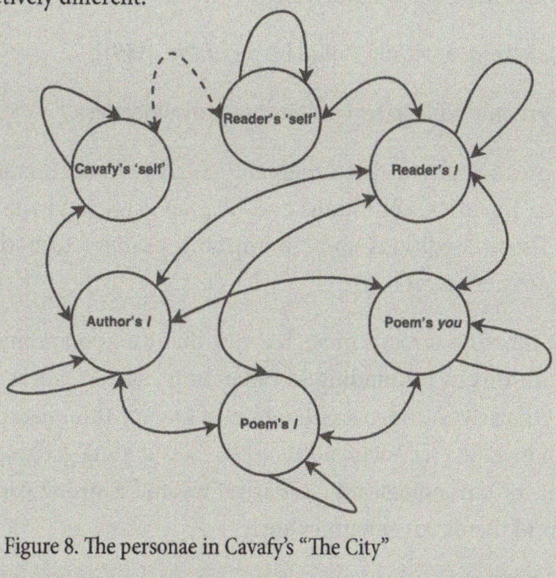

Figure 8. The personae in Cavafy's "The City"

---

1. Constantine P. Cavafy, *Poems: The Canon* (Cambridge, Mass.: Harvard Early Modern and Modern Greek Library, 2011), 2; my translation from the Greek.

(though almost entirely unrelated) political contexts dominated by strong and pyramidal power, poetic competition, and the institution of the court—entire sets of prescriptions sought to determine the tone and content of some poetic genres, as could be seen with the very official debates in Paris surrounding tragedies or with the rules on the "seasonal" themes of Edo chained poetry. Generic specialization, with its requirement for perlocutionary success, interferes with expression.

2.16.2 There may be no *theme* in poetry—no *given* external category that would simply be *put* or *couched* in a text. The literary performance of a "theme" makes it a nontheme that is a singular entity entangled in the poetics of the text and a shifter for thinking. I prefer speaking of *notions* to designate *what* is said poetically. Notions are both reflexive operators and quasi-concepts, sonically and semantically (de)formed. Sever them from the enunciative space that shapes them, then treat them as nondiscursive and prerational structures, as figments of the imagination or of the collective unconscious, as psychoanalytic complexes or subjective obsessions, and you will have "themes." [[48]]

2.16.3 Notions are shortcuts to reflexivity.

2.16.3.0 Once poeticized, any *thing* could be recursive. [[49]]

2.16.4 Notions are not subjective. Notions are not subjectless.

2.16.5 Notions are mental constructs mapping experience onto literature. Of course, historical conditions and biographical circumstances matter. Those conditions and circumstances *adhere* to notions; they do not transcend them.

2.16.6 We may construe notions in such a way that they communicate. Writers do this in responding to other texts, as do readers who engage themselves in the proliferation of literary thinking. Once we begin juxtaposing poetic notions notwithstanding geographic, linguistic, or chronological boundaries, we find a strong convergence amid thematic unboundedness.

2.16.7 Admittedly, the commonalities of human existence partially explain the convergence of notions. With other mammals we have in common an emotional circuitry, the reality of sexual reproduction,

48. *A notion in Coleridge's "The Rime of the Ancient Mariner."*

Death is not a *theme* in "The Rime of the Ancient Mariner": Coleridge does not "conjure up" death; he *meditates* on it, as intensely as a philosopher would do, but through notions rather than concepts ("Is that a DEATH? and are there two?").[1] Then, death is not only represented in the text; it is also presented as in the duet of disembodied voices in the penultimate part of "The Rime," recounting how the "lifeless and flat"[2] corpses of the crew are suddenly animated by the "seraph-band":

> No voice did they impart—
> No voice; but oh! the silence sank
> Like music on my heart.[3]

Notions are not plain concepts either, if by this term we seek to refer to well-circumscribed ideas that have been normalized through definitions or to the philosopher's creation and *organon*. There are too many deaths in Coleridge's "DEATH," too many impossibilities and contradictions, for any nomothetic idea to thrive. Throughout the poetic process, the conceptualization of *death* is performed and irremediably deformed. The untenability of the concept, allied to its intellective existence, brings forth notions.

---

1. Samuel Taylor Coleridge, *The Rime of the Ancient Mariner*, section III, line 188.
2. Ibid., section V, line 488.
3. Ibid., section V, lines 496–499.

our mortality. The human drive for describing and showing the natural and social environment is the root of so many texts—in most, if not all, cultures—about flora and fauna or about collective events such as wars.

All this is true, though not decisive enough. Geometric ornamentation, abstract figures, animals, human hands, and narrative episodes (hunts and, possibly, metamorphoses) are painted on the cave walls of Chauvet, Lascaux, and Altamira, but the representation of the human face is quite scarce. We do not doubt that prehistoric artists were anatomically, cognitively, and symbolically very similar to "us"; they were obviously familiar with human faces. The hypothesis of a taboo on representation remains unconvincing, given the very large timeline and the presence of a few portraits. All in all, we can only suppose that *drawing* a visage was not so signifi-

49. *The specularity of things in Francis Ponge.*

The potential specularity of anything within a poem is a key lesson of Francis Ponge's *Le parti pris des choses*. "The oyster" • "L'huître" could serve as an emblem for the whole collection: "It is a stubbornly closed world" • "c'est un monde opiniâtrement clos" that one must open after multiple attempts and in which "one finds a whole world . . . under a *firmament* (properly speaking)" • "on trouve tout un monde . . . sous un *firmament* (à proprement parler)."[1] Here, "properly speaking" implies both the use of all the strata of language (including the reactivation of the etymological sense of *firmament*)[2] and the exploitation of linguistic recursion. There is no a priori limit to reflexivity. "The wild blackberries" • "Les mûres" are to be found along the roads, and so are poems, those "typographic bushes" • "buissons typographiques."[3] The very last sentences of the *Parti pris* allow an etymological pun on the name of the *stone* that was examined (in the form of a pebble) as well as metapoetic considerations on the author's style and its critiques: "mes critiques diront: 'Ayant entrepris d'écrire une description de la pierre, il s'empêtra.'" • "my critiques will say: 'Having endeavored to write a description of the rock, he was then on the rocks.'"[4] For Ponge, every thing is reflexive of the poetic becoming of all things and is, once voiced, undeniably metallegorical in function, if not in nature.

1. Francis Ponge, *Œuvres complètes* (Paris: Gallimard, 1998), 1:21; my translation from the French.

2. See the explanation given by Ponge himself in *Entretiens de Francis Ponge avec Philippe Sollers* (Paris: Gallimard, 1970), 144.

3. Ponge, *Œuvres complètes*, 1:17.

4. Ibid., 1:56. Before Littré especially, the French verb *s'empêtrer* • *to become ensnared* was often thought to be derived from the Latin *in petra* and was thus etymologically linked to *pierre* • *stone*.

cant for those human populations, despite their "nature" and our attested reliance on facial expression in social life.

In poetry, content inclusion and exclusion cannot merely *mirror* biological and social experience. Cross cultural convergence of notions makes us wonder if some topics are deemed to be more universally *attuned* to poetry than others. If such were the case, and once we discard social framing and upend "human nature" as a unique explanation, we are left with a noetic source. Some notions may be better to think through poetically because other forms of speech are lacking. What epistemic and prescriptive discourses fail to explain could be addressed by the poem, for even its failure would give way to signification—whereas gaps or deadends in chemistry, philosophy, politics, divination, or theology are constitutively problematic. Verses in predictions, prayers, or physics serve as safeguards against self-defeat.

Then, even when an object or feeling (like the moon or sorrow) is comprehensively explained by organized knowledge (like astronomy or psychology), the experience *of* it remains largely untouched. "What is it like to be a bat?" is a question addressed to philosophers, neurologists, and biologists. A poetic answer might aid us best.

2.16.8 Of the things that we perceive and that happen to us, the incomprehensible, the unknown, the unexplainable, and the irreducible all command the *poeticity* of notions.

2.16.8.0 "Poeticity" is a *husteron proteron*, a textual recurring trait that is reterritorialized on the world. Poetry is "saying the unsayable," *when* and *if* it relates itself to the real, and shifts its qualities to the latter.

2.16.8.1 Along with structured reiteration and vivid imagery, poeticity accounts for the impression of finding "poetry" beyond, or beside, linguistic objects. So is the poetry of Rezo Gabriadaze's puppet shows *Stalingrad* and *The Autumn of Our Springtime*, of Sergei Parajanov's movies *Shadows of Forgotten Ancestors* and *The Color of Pomegranates,* of the double pages from Katsushika Hokusai's *Manga* transfiguring cloudy, snowy, smoky or misty landscapes. Should one rather say *poesy*?

2.16.8.2 Poetry does not *have* to address *poeticity*.

2.16.8.3 Poetry says the mystery of things and life without renouncing the mystery.

2.16.9 *Topoi* are identifiable but flexible associations of motifs, figures, words, and notions that speech *reiterates*. Variations—even slight ones—are indispensable; without them, a topos is a cliché. In some eras and regions, topoi are highly valued, and poetic *inventio* requires the mastery of a vast repertoire. In such contexts, the topical partakes in regulative repetition. At the opposite end, purely atopic poetry barely exists, for the most groundbreaking text could be (and will be) related to *comparanda* by its readers or could open up a new tradition. *Lettrisme*, whose poems were based on letters (neither words nor sounds), soon became a registry for itself.

2.16.9.0 *Phrases*—understood as discursive matrices, full of parlance, topoi, and argumentative lineaments holding speech—are stratified historical constructs with political underpinnings. When found in poetry, *phrases* work as tacit and concrete subregulation, with some texts reproducing readymade expression and others being eventful.

2.16.9.1 Topos is for *koinos topos*. The identifiable core is *common*. Variation is *shared*. "Common places" are relays of social institutions and cognitive conduits for the mind: Participants in the performance are being guided, and their noetic pace is quickened by their level of familiarity with the material. Now, topical variation is the intellective part, as rhythm emerging from meter, as exception intersecting rule. [[50]]

2.16.9.2 Like notions, topoi are necessary, though not restricted, to poetic thinking.

2.16.9.3 *Types* are transcultural. They concern characters (the sidekick, the villain, the noble king), situations (being lost in a hostile environment, taking refuge in a cave), motifs (shapeshifting, turning a dangerous situation to one's own benefit), or narrative structures (the quest, coming back empty-handed after a journey). Types often fetch topoi, but a difference should be marked between those two kinds of generalities. Types look like *imprints* of basic acculturation. Both Freud's and Jung's psychoanalytic theories were invested in harvesting those supposedly mental imprints and archetypes. Research on folktales, on a narrower basis, tried to collect "fundamentals" as well. Northrop Frye conjectured the existence of "a group of universal symbols . . . common to all men," like "those of food and drink, of the quest or journey, of light and darkness, and of sexual fulfillment," which would become consolidated "inside the mind" as "archetypal universal symbols."[23]

The material and mental commonalities of early development might in fact create a *typology* we respond to—as, I believe, other apes do. Claiming that poetry (or the arts) would be more typological (or closer to the unconscious) than other human endeavors would be purely phraseological, and worthless.

2.16.9.4 *Phrases* and *types* are possible *conditions* for notions and topoi: no origin, no explanation. [[51]]

50. *Ernst Robert Curtius and the transhistorical dimension of topoi.*

Ernst Robert Curtius saw the topical as the cement of a discursive edifice. European medieval literature had something *in common*, on which it built itself, the philologist argued. Yet, what happens if we isolate some reputedly European topoi and find them to be operative in nonrelated traditions? The old category of "influence" does not work; theories on the "last common ancestor" would look farfetched; the unity of human life is dubious. Is there a mental grammar of the possible? A closed number of element permutations? A series of irrelevant coincidences? Or are we, by the very fact of registering topoi, creating technical artifacts that we confuse with results?

Curtius is not always clear on the status of his central category. His hypothesis is obviously historicist, as it claimed that the Latin—and later medieval—reworking of Greek rhetoric constituted "data banks" for forms: "There is one tradition that goes from the Roman second bloom ca. 400 to the Renaissance of the twelfth century, and from there to the baroque."[1] The reality of "schools of rhetoric" in late antiquity and in the new European universities is, for Curtius, a key factor in the historical development he calls the "rhetoricization of poetics."[2] Nonetheless, Curtius also makes reference to Jung.[3] He claims that the topical strengthens "our understanding of the Western history of the soul,"[4] while noticing en passant that the motif of the *puer senex*, for instance, could be found outside of Europe, in the Bible or in ancient Sanskrit texts.[5]

Then, what would a "poetic topos" be? Curtius first answers through a series of "themes" (the beauty of nature, awe, dreaming, love, friendship, the past) that are both "timeless"[6] and "historical." He later gives "the call to nature" as a paradigm.[7] In our terms, the poeticity of some notions would depend on the inexplicable (the alchemy of affects, the surprise in front of the unknowable), the incommensurable (individual human life in cosmos and *phusis*), or the inexorable (time and death), that is, on experiences resisting rational and instrumental reducibility. Subsequent topoi both amplify and specify notions. They are recognizable units that could be diffracted again.

---

1. Ernst Robert Curtius, "Begriff einer historischen Topik" (1938), in *Topoforschung*, ed. Max L. Baeumer (Darmstadt: Wissenschaftliche Buchgesellschaft, 1973), 12; my translation from the German.

2. See ibid., 11, and Ernst Robert Curtius, *Europäische Literatur und lateinisches Mittelalter* (Bern: Francke, 1948), 77.

3. Curtius, *Europäische Literatur*, 90.

4. Ibid., 90.

5. Ibid., 107, 107n1.

6. Ibid., 90.

7. Ibid., 99–102.

51. *Some examples of transcultural topoi (on "nature").*

Curtius's "call to nature" is a general rubric for topical associations across cultures, all serving the purpose of channeling the poetic. I find apostrophes to the sun in ancient Egyptian odes, in Ajax's farewell to life, in an Incan prayer reported by Cristóbal de Molina, or in *Paradise Lost.*

jnḏ-ḥr≠k jtn n hrw qmꜣ tm jr ꜥnḫ≠sn bjk ꜥꜣ
sꜣb šwt ḫprr sṯs sw ḏs≠f ḫpr ḏs≠f jwtj ms.tw≠f

•

Hail to you, celestial disk of the day, creator of all who make them live, great falcon, brightly plumed, beetle [*or*: BsR] who raised himself, who created himself, who wasn't created.

(Egyptian hymn to the Sun)[1]

Sù d', ō̂ tòn aipun ouranòn diphrēlatō̂n
Hḗlie, patrọ̄́an tḕn emḕn hótan khthóna
ídẹ̄s, episkhṑn khrusónōton hēnían
ággeilon átas tàs emàs móron t' emòn
géronti patrì tẹ̄̂ te dustḗnọ̄ trophọ̄̂.

•

O you, driving the chariot in the steep skies,
O Sun, when you'll see my fatherland,
pull on the gold-studded reins, and
announce my doom, my fate to my
old father and wretched nurturer.

(Sophocles)[2]

Uiracochaya
"Punchao cachunto, tacachun,"
nispac nic . . .
Casilla quispilla punchao Iynga

•

Lord Wiracocha,
Who says
"Let there be day, let there be night!" . . .
Shine on your Inca people.

(Incan prayer)[3]

O Sun, to tell thee how I hate thy beams
That bring to my remembrance from what state

I fell, how glorious once above thy Spheare

(Milton)[4]

Beyond apostrophes, that nature could inspire the poet's introspection is certainly not the late, romantic, invention some Western scholars talk about. The contemplation of the moon elicits melancholy or the evocation of inner feelings in writings by Li Bai, Rumi, Brentano, and García Lorca alike.

靜夜思
床前明月光
疑是地上霜
舉頭望明月
低頭思故鄉
"Jìng yè sī"
Chuáng qián míng yuè guāng
yí shì dì shàng shuāng
jǔ tóu wàng míng yuè
dī tóu sī gù xiāng
•
"Quiet Night Thoughts"
In front of my bed, the bright shine of the moon:
I mistake it for frost on the ground.
I raise my head, I look at the bright moon;
I lower my head, I think of my old home.

(Li Bai)[5]

Ke-andîshed ze roy-è Mah hejâb ast hejâb
Del chon Mâh ast, dar del andîshed madâr
•
Thoughts are veils that hide the moon's bright face.
The heart's a moon, where thinking has no place.

(Rumi)[6]

Hier spinn' ich so allein
Der Mond scheint klar und rein,
Ich sing' und möchte weinen.
•
Here I weave alone,
The moon shines, clear and pure,
I sing and would like to cry.

(Brentano)[7]

Cuando sale la luna
de cien rostros iguales,
la moneda de plata
solloza en el bolsillo.

•

When the moon rises
with a hundred equal faces,
the silver coin
sobs in the pocket.

(García Lorca)[8]

The fate of the most beautiful flowers is a pretext to meditate on the transience of human life or love for Qu Yuan, Ono no Komachi, Pierre de Ronsard, and in the Hebraic Psalms. In the Arabo-Persian world, the topos even forms a vast subgenre, the *zahriyyât*, that has been studied in its own right.[9]

ʾŭnōš kᵊ≠[h]a≠ḥaṣīr yam-a(y)≠w kᵊ≠ṣīṣ ha≠śadā̆ kin yaṣiṣ
kī rūḥ ʿabårā b≠ō wᵊ≠ʾēn-an≠[h]u(w) wᵊ≠lō(ʾ) yakkīr-an≠[h]u(w) ʿōd måqōm≠ō

•

Man, his days are like grass, ¦ like a wild flower, so he flowers.
If a wind passes over him, he is no more ¦ and his home knows him no longer

(Psalms)[10]

余既滋蘭之九畹兮 . . .
哀眾芳之蕪穢 . . .
老冉冉其將至兮
yú jì zī lán zhī jiŭ wăn xi . . .
āi zhòng fāng zhī wú huì . . .
lăo răn răn qí jiāng zhì xi

•

I had tended many an acre of orchids . . .
I grieve to see these blossoms waste in rank weeds . . .
Old age comes creeping and soon will be upon me

(Qu Yuan)[11]

花の色はうつりにけりないたづらにわが身世にふるながめせしまに
Hana no iro wa utsurinikeri na itazura ni wa ga mi yo ni furu nagame seshi ma ni

•

A life in vain. My looks, talents faded like these cherry blossoms paling in the endless rains that I gaze out upon, alone.

(Ono no Komachi)[12]

Cueillez cueillez vostre jeunesse:
Comme à ceste fleur la vieillesse
Fera ternir vostre beauté.

•

Pluck, pluck your youth:
As with this flower, old age
Will tarnish your beauty.

(Ronsard)[13]

In each "tradition," innumerable other examples could be mentioned, and intertextual quotations abound, which shows the deliberate recourse to well-known structures of thought in order to address the unknowable. However, posing that each poem is "a repeat"[14] or "only varies a typical form within the tradition"[15] is unwarranted, since echoes are not limited to outright "ascendancies" within a cultural area.

---

1. Adriaan de Buck, *Egyptian Readingbook* (Chicago: Ares, 1948), 113–115; I am using De Buck's translation, with a slight correction. I am reproducing the transliteration prepared by Mark-Jan Nederhof, https://mjn.host.cs.st-andrews.ac.uk/egyptian/texts/corpus/pdf/HymnSun.pdf.

2. Sophocles, *Ajax*, lines 845–849; my translation from the Greek.

3. John Curl, ed. and trans., *Ancient American Poets* (Tempe: Bilingual Press, 2005), 137. The text appears in Cristóbal de Molina, *Relación de las fábulas y ritos de los Incas* (Lima: Universidad de San Martin de Porres, 2008), 69–70 (with a different transliteration).

4. John Milton, *Paradise Lost*, book IV, lines 37–39.

5. *Quan Tang shi* (Beijing: Zhonggua shuju, 1960), 5:165.1709; my translation from the Chinese.

6. Rumi, *Kolliyaat-e Shams-e Tabrizi*, trans. Zara Houshmand, poem 84, https://iranian.com/Arts/Rumi/84.html.

7. Clemens Brentano, *Werke* (Munich: Hanser, 1968), 1:131 ("Der Spinnerin Nachtlied," lines 22–24); my translation from the German.

8. Federico García Lorca, *Obras completas* (Madrid: Aguilar, 1980), 1:339 ("La luna asoma," *Canciones*); my translation from the Spanish.

9. See Gregor Schoeler, *Arabische Naturdichtung* (Beirut: Orient-Institut der deutschen Morgenländischen Gesellschaft, 1974).

10. *Psalms* 103:15–16. I am reproducing the scholarly transliteration prepared by Wolfgang Richter, *Biblia Hebraica transcripta* (St. Ottilien: Eos, 1991–93), 11:406–408, and the translation by Mitchell Dahood, *Psalms III: 101–150* (New York: Doubleday, 1970), 23–24.

11. Qu Yuan, "On Encountering Trouble," lines 49, 56, 63, translated by Fusheng Wu (with modifications) in Zong-Qi Cai, *How to Read Chinese Poetry*, 44–45.

12. *Ogura Hyakunin Isshu*, poem 9. I am giving the translation of Peter McMillan in his *One Hundred Poets: One Poem Each* (New York: Columbia University Press, 2010), 11.

13. Pierre de Ronsard, *Œuvres complètes* (Paris: Gallimard, 1993), 1:673 [*Odes*, book I, poem 17]; my translation from the French.

14. Helen Vendler, *Poems, Poets, Poetry: An Introduction and Anthology* (Boston: Bedford, 1997), 619.

15. Curtius, "Begriff einer historischen Topik," 15; my translation from the German.

52. *Some classes of topoi associated with poetic genres.*

Dirges on the wretched destiny of the captives appear in Euripides's *Women of Troy*, François Villon's *Testament*, or the Quechua *harawi* compiled by Waman Puma. The hyperbolic praise of rulers, winners, and warriors is equally expressed in the Olympic hymns, the panegyrics of Sidonius Apollinaris, *The Secret History of the Mongols*, the Korean *Songs of Flying Dragons*, the Ottoman *kaside*, or Vladimir Mayakovsky's *Vladimir Ilich Lenin*. The derision of moral or physical deformity is found in Juvenal's *Satires*, the subgenre of *contre-blason*, improvised verbal attacks against an opponent in the Cypriot *tsiattista*, or some *Hassaniya* songs from Mali.[1]

1. Here is an example of a *Hassaniya* satire: "ʕand-ak z-zwaymal gayyam lə-briiħ | wa-ẓq̣aṭ zaađ f-kulli žiih-a | kuun t-ħull-ii-ha lə-r-riiħ | w-laa łaahi t-riiħ-i fii-ha" • "Your vagina raised a roar. | It shouted more in all directions. | Unless you untie it to the wind, | You'll have no rest from it." Excerpt from a text given by informant B in 1989 to Jeffrey Heath, trans., *Hassaniya Arabic (Mali): Poetic and Ethnographic Texts* (Wiesbaden: Harrassowitz, 2003), 20–21.

2.16.9.5 Among the most widespread poetic topics are also those that are taken within the brackets of the genres. Laments and praises, satires and prayers, curses and charms, catalogues, and beast fables, as well as other similar speech forms, are closely associated with songs and verses throughout human history, inducing commonplaces. [[52]]

2.16.9.6 The intellective share of poetry selects the same topoi across cultures for the potential they offer to self-commenting and transconsistence. [[53]]

2.16.10 Topoi are regulative expansions of notions. Relying on proliferation and ordered reiteration, their *tekhnē* immediately becomes

53. *Examples of reflexive and transcultural topoi.*

The preterition of the ineffable, the pregnant fiction of dreams, and the singing of birds are extensively referred to across cultural borders and historical periods. Intoxication deserves a consideration of its own. Baudelaire's prose poem and command "Enivrez-vous" ("Get drunk") is a response to what may be the most universal reflexive topic of poetry. While brief songs could be improvised on the spot, at the occasion of a ceremony or banquet, most texts dealing with the inspiration of drugs or alcohol are in fact written or composed by authors while sober. The subjective experience of "poetic rapture" is being repeatedly, and recursively, linked with the altered consciousness brought by "artificial paradises." Apart from romantic intoxication and the intense celebration of drugs in the lyrics of contemporary pop, rock, and rap music, the poetic depiction of various "substance abuse," encompassing plenitude, gaiety, hallucination, or ecstasy, is the backbone of several large, often disconnected and enduring, bodies of texts. In the multitude of works from the Arabo-Persian world, Hafez and Abu Nuwas are exemplary, and they also influenced Jewish writers from Egypt, Andalusia, and the Maghreb. Japanese songs from the most ancient anthologies extoll the qualities of wine drinking, and inebriation is a hallmark of Chinese *shi*.

Among the most ancient written poems (second millennium BCE) are a Sumerian hymn to Ninkasi, the beer goddess, as well as many Sanskrit *vedas* on *soma*, a drug that has been variedly interpreted as cannabis or as an entheogenic plant. The *Rigveda* includes a hymn where the *I* (a sage or a god) praises his own inspiration, with the refrain "Have I not drunk soma?" • "kuvit somasyāpām iti." The *I* also says: "like impetuous winds, the drinks have lifted me up" • "pra vātā iva dodhata un mā pītā ayaṃsata" and "The prayer [*or*: hymn] has come to me as a lowing cow comes to her beloved son" • "upa mā matir asthita vāśrā putram iva priyam."[1] Another recursive *veda* associates the poetic inspiration by intoxication with the sound of the stones extracting the *soma* juice, while repeating the lexical root *vad* (referring to speech or to sound): "Praite vadantu pra vayaṃ vadāma ghrāvabhyo vācaṃ vadatāvadadbhyaḥ" • "Let them raise their voices, and let us raise our voices. Speak your speech to the stones that speak."[2] And, of course, topoi similarly speak to one another, holding the power of *enchanting* the real.

---

1. *Rig veda*, 10:119; Wendy Doniger's translation (Harmondsworth: Penguin, 1981).
2. Ibid., 10:94.

self-reflexive in poetry. They virtually inscribe endless repetition in both the *saying* and the *said*. There, topoi are constitutively close to poetic devices. They are an easy vector for the "poeticization of rhetoric."

2.16.11 "Poetic" topoi and notions are the highly complex outcomes of many factors, including *psychological typology* (possibly a genetic and epigenetic imprint), social use (through insertion in a context of enunciation, like a festival, a ritual, a collective event), mnemonic consolidation (with topoi and formulas easing the composition of oral poetry, pedagogical transmission reinforcing repetition and variation, intertextual memory building up a tradition), *discursive conditions* (in the interplay of modes and moods, given the co-option of topics by formal systems of reiteration, with thematic fixation through genres), the *noetic dimensions of the human experience* (where phenomena such as the communicational will to describe the world, path dependency, language defection and semantics, or recursive metacognition are paving the way toward the intellective rendition of qualia, of the incommensurable, of the nonrational, of the unthinkable), and *metapoetic self-selection* (when the reflexive feature of notions and commonplaces is more easily incorporated, through the proximity to poetic processes of mental perceptions like dreaming or altered consciousness). Each of those factors may come to us with a built-in history—affixed to political settings, to specific genres, to the threads of traditions, etc.—but not only are they transhistorical as such; they also depend on mechanisms and orders of consequence that defy the usual timeline of social groups.

2.17 *Poetry suggests "thinking experiments" for the unthinkable.*

2.17.0 We gain ideas by speculating. As Ernst Mach once argued, literature is filled with "thought experiments," concerning all the things we do not know yet or will ever ignore.[24] Each world of fiction is a possible (or, if inconsistent, impossible) world. The humblest story could give "food for thought," in asking us both to assess the merits and plausibility of the tale and to imagine what others would have done in the same situation. The elaboration of characters or description of affects tap into our mental aptitude for empathy and

54. *A thought experiment in Marie de France's "Bisclavret."*

The Breton lay of Bisclavret told in Anglo-Norman by Marie de France is a case study about a werewolf—and about betrayal. The wife of Bisclavret, after learning that her husband is a lupine shapeshifter, prevents him from returning to his human form by hiding his clothes. She then marries her lover and accomplice. During a hunt a year later, the wolf-baron implores clemency from the king, who is amazed by the odd behavior of the wild animal (who, crying for mercy, "kisses [the king's] leg and foot" • "la jambe li baise e le pié")[1] and decides to keep it with him at his castle. The adulterous wife and her new spouse are separately recognized by Bisclavret, who tries to attack them. He succeeds at biting off the nose of his spouse. The aggression stands in such contrast with the usual temperament of the wolf that the king and his court soon suspect there is a reason for Bisclavret's reactions. The wife finally confesses, and the baron recovers his human clothes—and original form.

The lay is a practical reflection on retribution and on the consequences of infidelity. It confronts us with the feelings associated to betrayal, vengeance, and "rage." It is also a lesson in interpreting the signs of the external world. "A wise man" • "un sages huem"[2] at the court suspects that the wolf's ire might be linked to the disappearance of the baron. Marie amusingly ends her tale by saying that the infamous mark of the punished wife has been transmitted to her descendants:

> plusurs des femmes del lignage,
> c'est veritez, senz nes sunt nees
> e si viveient esnasees.
> •
> several women of that lineage,
> 'tis truth, were born with no nose
> and so they lived denosed.[3]

Physiognomy is hermeneutic. As for the metamorphosis of the werewolf, it encourages us to reconsider reality (and Brittany in particular) as being subject to *marvels* (*merveille* • *marvel* occurring six times over 318 lines). It also makes us feel what it is like to be a wolf (or a human trapped in the shape of a wolf) and raises the question of human animality. The insistence on *truth* at the end of the lay[4] is another part of the thought experiment: What happens if the unlikely or the marvelous are as true as ordinary experience? And what does truth mean, if this tale ever comes to be known as an invention? Beside its narrative, Marie's poem is a reservoir for such conjectures and considerations. This certainly explains the success of the piece, whose medieval avatars include its retelling by the Icelandic *Tiodels saga*.

---

1. Marie de France, "Bisclavret," line 148. My translation from the Anglo-Norman on the basis of the edition by Karl Warnke, *Lais de Marie de France* (Tübingen: Niemeyer: 1900), 75–85.

2. Ibid., line 239.

3. Ibid., lines 312–315. *Nees* • *born* and *nes* • *nose* are paronyms.

4. Ibid., lines 313, 316.

identification. Stronger alterations of the texture of the real (as in "fantastic" or utopian literature) offer a track toward *Gedankenexperiment*. [[54]]

2.17.1 The best poems are *thinking experiments* for the unthinkable. Along with other noetic excursions outside of the computable range, they suggest to us ways to think beyond the limits of thought.

2.17.1.0 Riddles are verbal puzzles, full of semantic ambiguities and inflexions, whose goal is to tease and disorient the listener (or the reader). They are often versified. Once they have been deciphered, their value is null, unless we appropriate them and ask friends to solve the problem ("do you know this one?"), which is in accordance with their social currency. *Thinking* experiments go further. [[55]]

2.17.1.1 The "unthinkable" could be the very stuff poems are made of. [[56]] [[57]]

55. *From riddle to thinking experiment in Gertrude Stein.*

The tenth-century Exeter manuscript compiles nearly a hundred poetic riddles in Old English. In living folk traditions that are still extant in Filipino or Bengali cultures, riddles use parallelism, rhymes, and alliterations, often in couplets or quatrains. Sanskrit literature offers what may be the most developed and sophisticated corpus of riddle-poems. Like other similar mental exercises, the playful component comes from surprise and problem solving, including a necessary "aha moment," without which the game participant just remains—precisely—puzzled. Western "modernist" poetry has been routinely treated as a high-grade puzzle—and it commonly elicits indifference or frustration among readers who try to find the key. In fact, some texts are little more than this. For instance, a four-line "portrait" of Guillaume Apollinaire written by Gertrude Stein begins with a baffling "Give known or pin ware," which the 1993 *Stein Reader* correctly interprets[1] as an admittedly loose phonetic approximation for the name of the French-Polish poet: [gɪvnoʊnɔrpɪnwɛr] for [gijo:m'apɔlinɛʀ], or, with a stronger American accent, for [gɪjoʊmæpɔlɪnɛr]. The last line recommends us to "leave eye" to the benefit of the "lessons" or "les sons" (*the sounds*, in French). Such a verbal, transidiomatic game is as interesting as a Sanskrit *prahelika* or a Duchamp readymade.

Another of Stein's short pieces—written, like the previous quatrain, in 1911 and similarly collected in the 1934 *Portraits and Prayers*—begins with:

> One, one, one, there are many of them. There are very many of them. There are many of them. Each one of them is one. Each one is one, there are many of them. Each one is one, there are many of them, there are very many of them. Each one is one, there are many of them.[2]

While this text is very different from the one I mentioned previously, the magazine *Rogue* that first printed it (in 1915) explained it as a riddle. Actually, this would be a rather transparent riddle, the solution being in the title (the name of the Parisian general store "Galeries Lafayette"). Throughout the few pages of the poem, Stein repeats the oscillating multiplicity and unicity of "each one" (each customer, each gallery, each item, each one) and repeats her own repetitions in a way that performs the one that is *one* and *many*. The conclusive paragraph reads:

> Each one is one and is that one and is especially that one and is that especial one and is accustomed to being that one, is used to being that one, is quite used to being that one, is very well accustomed to be that one, is certainly very well accustomed to be that especial one, is very well accustomed to be especially that one, is very well accustomed to be the one that one is being, is one that is being one and each

> one is one and there are many of them and each one is any one and any one is one, is an especial one, and each one is one, and there are many of them and each one is any one of them and any one of them is an especial one, and each one is one, each one is the one that is being that one, and each one is one, and each one is being the one each one is being, and each one is one, and each one is being each one, and each one is being the one each one is being, and each one is one is the one that one is being, each one is being one is one being the one that one is being. Each one is one. There are many of them. Each one is one. Each one is one being the especial one that one is being.[3]

There are undeniably algorithmic processes that move the text through recursive specifications, branching, integration. That is its machinery. When we read the whole poem, we lose track—of time, of what was said before, of what we are if we are one, and there are many of us, one that is being one, that one, or any one that is used to being that one, etc. Yet we think intellectively the oneness of the multiple and the multiplicity of the one (topics we can only philosophically touch upon, and maybe wrongly so, if one abides by Carnap's "destruction" of metaphysics) because we are, in fact, making our way through the prose poem. As I read the piece, I also prolong some sentences and bifurcate propositions (in the way I did in this paragraph). I am beginning to make mine a noetic—and poetic—device that is built within language and within English. For instance, that *that* would both be a demonstrative ("that one") and a relative pronoun ("the one that one is being"), that *one* would be a number ("one, one, one"), a pronoun ("the one that one"), and a quasi-adjective ("is one"), as well as the structures of the present progressive (allowing the *excipit* "is being"), are all linguistic properties of one idiom that has no systematic equivalents in other languages. The thinking experiment goes back to itself: Is it one and the same, if it only occurs *here*, in American English? Are we thinking what is, what it is to be, what it is to be one, what it is to be one being one, only through the transient and local experience of a set of idiomatic utterances? The philosophical revocation of logology cannot hide that, through poetic notions rather than concepts, we think what we cannot grasp cognitively or even contain within the disciplined positivity of ordered languages.

---

1. Ulla E. Dydo ed., *A Stein Reader* (Evanston, Ill.: Northwestern University Press, 1993), 278.
2. Gertrude Stein, *Portraits and Prayers* (New York: Random House, 1934), 169.
3. Ibid., 171–172.

56. *Naming the impossible in Euripides's* Medea *(ll. 1–10).*

The opening lines of Euripides's *Medea* briefly recast the events that led to the nascent tragedy through a series of counterfactual propositions.

> Eíth' ṓphel' Argoûs mḕ diaptásthai skáphos
> Kólkhōn es aîan kuanéas Sumplēgádas,
> mēd' en nápaisi Pēlíou peseîn pote
> tmētheîsa peúkē, mēd' eretmō̂sai khéras
> andrō̂n arístōn, hoì tò págkhruson déros
> Pelíạ metē̂lthon. Ou gàr àn déspoin' emḕ
> Mḗdeia púrgous gē̂s épleus' Iōlkías
> érōti thumòn ekplageîs' Iásonos:
> oud' àn ktaneîn peísasa Peliádas kóras
> patéra katọ̄kei tēnde gēn Korinthían
> •
> Would that the hull of swift Argo did not wing its way
> to the country of Colchis through the cyanean Symplegades,
> would that, in the dells of Pelion, the pine tree were never
> felled, giving no oars to the hands of the heroes who,
> at Pelias's command, sought up the Golden Fleece! My mistress,
> Medea, would not have come to the towers of the land of Iolcos,
> her heart stricken with love for Jason:
> she wouldn't have persuaded the daughters of Pelias to kill
> their father and she wouldn't inhabit this land of Corinth.[1]

The character is trying to obliterate the action fictitiously, by negating the past. The artificiality of such a set of hypotheses is underlined by the rather convoluted and initial expression "eíth' ṓphele": What happened did happen, but would that it were not the case! The nurse, who is speaking, is going backward, first imagining a universe where Argo would not reach Colchis, then even posing a world where the trees of Mount Pelion would not have been used for crafting the oars of the ship. In either scenario, Medea would not have fallen in love with Jason (whom she would not have met), she would not have exiled herself and accomplished the deeds of her legend, and she would not be in Corinth with a husband who is about to repudiate her. In other words, there would be nothing (more) to tell. This very paradoxical *incipit* summarizes "in the negative" the narrative elements that are central to the play while exhibiting the facticity of the story through its counterfactual analysis. It can only stop at some point and revoke itself as a fantasy, so that the play could begin (afresh). In parallel, the very lofty tone of the first six lines of the *expositio negativa* are superseded by a more conversational style.

Medea's exordium offers a stratified thought experiment on interlinked events (where factual progression remains a requirement of story and history). It also forms a reflexive consideration on the possibility of beginning a tragedy. The text that feigns to void itself is a complex variation on the liar's paradox: If the nurse's wish were to be realized, then she would not be on stage mentioning episodes that did not take place; since counterfactuals do not change the course of events, they say what actually happened by trying to efface or change the past. The thought experiment goes deeper into the matter of the plot, for the nurse disseminates the name of Medea (in Greek: *Mḗdeia*) before uttering it for the first time: *mḕ diaptásthai, mēd' en, mēd' eretmôsai, déspoin' emḗ,* immediately before *Mḗdeia*. The noun of the main character is being partially voiced several times before its first complete occurrence, mainly through the negation *mḕ,* which is grammatically ruled by the expression of a wish (with the infinitive). *Mḗdeia* is not only the one who *thinks* and *plans* (*mḗdetai*); she is also in charge of what can*not,* of what should *not* be done—and, yet, is accomplished.

1. Euripides, *Medea,* lines 1–10; my translation from the Greek.

57. The experience of the unthinkable in Gennadi Aygi's "yes—and poet."

Like many other texts written by Gennadi Aygi, "da i poet"[1] is overwhelming. This dense and intense piece could be approached as a fragmented *ars poetica* conjuring up the remnants of the "'tragic'" • "'tragičeckoe'" and of "lyricism" • "lirizm," the very names of the poet ("a poet" • "poèt," "another Poet" • "Poèt drugoj," "Pushkin") and his tools ("words" • "slova," "hymn" • "gimn," "song" • "pen'e," "murmur" • "šorox," "verse" • "stroka"). The text begins with the differing values attributed to the same situation: Someone is "seemingly waiting for murderers" • "kak budto ždet ubijc"—while this is "tedious" • "skučno" here, it would be "'tragic'" • "'tragičeckoe'" elsewhere. The social, moral, aesthetic divergences prepare a reconsideration of both poetry and the real. There is "no Vastness here for saying: '*such a thing*' | through things or appearances" • "Ogromnosti tut net čtoby skazat': '*takoe*' | čerez javlenija il' vešči." Or, rather, as suggested by the indirect quote of another (unnamed) writer, the act of saying uses the "puppets" • "kukly" of "things or appearances" • "javlenija il' vešči" that are "—words" • "—slova." The last stanza distinguishes between "Reality Illumined" • "Real'nost' Osijannaja" (as "such—for the self . . .—is lyricism" • "takaja—dlja sebja . . .—lirizm") and "the poverty-masterpiece" • "niščenstvo-šedevr," having its own "*such*" • "*takoe*." Both "*such*" and "*such a thing*" translate the same Russian "*takoe*," *suchness* maybe. As with the other poetic modes mentioned earlier, a distinction is at work, but the first words of the last quatrain are "and yes" • "čto da," followed by a colon: The two paths are ruled by a *yes* that is now uttered a fourth time (including the occurrence in the title). It is as if this insisting *yes* were here to signify a poetic act going beyond position, negation, and assertion. This *yes* would not be Derrida's preoriginary assent but the *yessing* inherent in poetic affirmation, capable of calling up to our minds contradictory and impossible multitudes, here and now.

In such an affirmation, the poet as a puppet master is juxtaposed with the absent poet who does not pay the bill (through a reference to the proverbial Russian "joke: 'will Pushkin | pay for you too?'" • "anekdot: 'čto—Puškin | za vas zaplatit?'") and with the poets "perishing | in a new way: without words | and this—is their Poetry" • "gibnuščie | po-novomu: bez slov | i èto—ix Poèzija." Thanks to the art of the poet (of the *I*? of "another poet?"), the word *puppet* (*kukla*) is integrated as such into the puppet-words of the poem: *howl* becoming "puppethowl" • "voj kukol'nyj" and *wolves* "wolves-puppets" • "volki-kukly." In Russian, those words howl or rather sing; listen to them: "voj kukol'nyj | i volki-kukly." In contrast, "wolves-non-words *work* | and death-non-word will be" • "volki-ne-slova *rabotajut* | i budet smert'-ne-slovo," the words say. . . . In this quest for the *poor* verbal description of minimal suchness, poetic "'duty'" • "'dolg'" is not illuminating reality; it is not "un-covering" it. Poetry may lead "the *empty*—into *emptiness*" • "*pustoe*—v *pustotu*" and express the murmur of silent objects (the one of "the *Sun*" • "*Solnce*," the one of "the wall" • "stena") through the silence of language and the "voicelessly sighing | vestige of emptiness and deathliness" • "bezglasno vydoxnuv | ostatkom pustoty i mertvizny." And as if "such things" were not already so difficult to fathom, the event of the poem consists in saying and making all this, *at the same time*: Via the performance of the text, the poet is "without words" in the elliptic line of dots following "oh yes," a bit before the center of the text:

"o da
......................."

Words are as much puppet-words as they are words-non-words. Reality is illumined in retrospect and already humming like a wall or the Sun. The emptiness of death has never been so empty, while being strong and pliable as "iron" • "železo" (last word). I cannot be certain of what I just tried to understand. But yes, I may be sure there is even more.

---

1. I am using the bilingual ed. of Gennadi Aygy, *Selected Poems: 1954–1994*, trans. Peter France (Evanston, Ill.: Northwestern University Press, 1997), 128–131. I am retaining France's translation, with modifications. Thanks to Nancy Pollack and Dragan Kujundzic for their help with the Russian.

3 What one cannot compute, one must poetize, and think.

NOTES

PREFACE

1. Laurent Dubreuil, "What Is Literature's Now?" *New Literary History* 38, no. 1 (2007): 43–70; "On Experimental Criticism," *diacritics* 39, no. 1 (2009): 3–23; "On Poetry and Mind," *diacritics* 43, no. 1 (2015): 64–80; *De l'attrait à la possession* (Paris: Hermann, 2003); *L'état critique de la littérature* (Paris: Hermann, 2009); *The Empire of Language*, trans. David Fieni (Ithaca, N.Y.: Cornell University Press, 2013); *The Intellective Space: Thinking Beyond Cognition* (Minneapolis: University of Minnesota Press, 2015).

2. Others have recently stressed the particular role of poetry vis-à-vis the economic and political apparatus of late capitalism; see Christopher Nealon, *The Matter of Capital: Poetry and Crisis in the American Century* (Cambridge, Mass.: Harvard University Press, 2011); Jasper Bernes, *The Work of Art in the Age of Deindustrialization*, PhD diss., University of California–Berkeley (2012); or, to a lesser extent, Martin Rueff, *Différence et identité: Michel Deguy, situation d'un poète lyrique à l'apogée du capitalisme culturel* (Paris: Hermann, 2009). I might also refer to Marc Kohlbry, who works along the same line and is currently engaged in a PhD dissertation under my supervision at Cornell. I do not necessarily share the methodic approach of these authors (in relation to history, in particular), and I am drawing different consequences, but all those endeavors are worth exploring.

3. During the preparation of this research project, I had several decisive conversations with Laurent Ferri, Sue Savage-Rumbaugh, and Haiping Yan. I also relied on the generous expertise, patience, passion, and knowledge of many others, including Neal Allar, Marc Aymes, Bruno Bosteels, Morten Christiansen, Walter Cohen, Jean-Louis Dessalles, Pedro Erber, Joseph Fridman, Alexandre François, Mitchell Greenberg, Sylvère Guiriec, Marianne Hopman, Junting Huang, Matthew Kibbee, Richard Klein, Dragan Kujundzic, Tom McEnaney, Gerard de Melo, Xi Murong, Nancy Pollak, Pietro Pucci, Alessia Ricciardi, Antoine Saillenfest, Naoki Sakai, Marie-Claire Vallois, William West, and Dagmawi Woubshet. In the summer of 2015, Léa Polverini provided assistance for some exploratory aspects of the research.

I am very much indebted to all the participants of the "Poetry and Mind" seminar I conducted at Cornell University in the spring semester of 2015. I also thank the students and colleagues who attended the miniseminar sessions I gave in April 2015 and November 2016 at Tsinghua University. In both schools, the rich discussions I had with the audience have been essential for shaping and furthering my hypotheses. I have otherwise benefitted from the questions and observations I received during the discussions following my university lecture at Tsinghua in April 2015, the talk I delivered at the "Textual Objects" conference at Cornell in April 2016, and my presentation at Northwestern University in May 2016.

The very helpful comments and feedback provided to me by Diane Brown, Tristan Garcia, Brian Lennon, Jacques Lezra, Paul North, and Thomas Pavel on various drafts of this essay made the process of writing and revising the manuscript a much easier task. My very warm thanks go to the two alacritous and anonymous reviewers of this work and the production team at Fordham University Press. Neal Allar and Laurent Ferri have been the first readers of this book.

Finally, *Poetry and Mind* would not have been possible without the work and insights of, literally, hundreds of scholars from the past and the present era. I cannot do justice to all the authors and researchers I owe something, but I think readers will be able to "connect the dots" relatively easily. In a handful of less obvious cases, I added some bibliographic information, though, overall, endnotes are deliberately scarce, and their content is limited to a minimum.

1

1. On all this, see Laurent Dubreuil and Sue Savage-Rumbaugh, *Dialogues on the Human Ape* (Minneapolis: University of Minnesota Press, 2018).

2. Aristotle, *Poetics*, 1447b.

3. Gary Marcus, "Steamrolled by Big Data," *The New Yorker*, March 29, 2013.

2

1. About literature's response, see Laurent Dubreuil, "What Is Literature's Now?".

2. Johann Wolfgang von Goethe, *Sämtliche Werke* (Frankfort: Deutscher Klassiker Verlag, 1999), 39:50; my translation from the German.

3. Ibid.

4. Natalie Phillips, "Literary Neuroscience and History of the Mind," in *The Oxford Handbook of Cognitive Literary Studies*, ed. Lisa Zunshine (Oxford: Oxford University Press, 2015), 55–81.

5. Jan Mukařovský, *On Poetic Language* (Lisse: Peter de Ridder, 1976), 66–67.

6. Mark Turner, *Reading Minds: The Study of English in the Age of Cognitive Science* (Princeton, N.J.: Princeton University Press, 1991), 239.

7. Aristotle, *Rhetoric*, III, 2, 6; *Poetics*, 22.

8. See Aniruddh Patel, *Music, Language, and the Brain* (Oxford: Oxford University Press, 2008), 283.

9. W. Tecumseh Fitch, "The Biology and Evolution of Rhythm: Unravelling a Paradox," in *Language and Music as Cognitive Systems*, ed. Patrick Rebuchat et al. (Oxford: Oxford University Press, 2012), 73–109.

10. Plutarch, *On the Glory of the Athenians* [*De gloria Atheniensium*], 346F; my translation from the Greek.

11. Ibid., 347C.

12. Horace, *Poetic Art*, line 361.

13. On "poeticizing" and "romanticizing" the world, see Novalis, *Werke* (Munich: Hanser, 1978–1987), esp. 1:397, 2:362–364, 2:488.

14. Gerard Manley Hopkins, *Journals and Papers* (Oxford: Oxford University Press, 1959), 84; Roman Jakobson, *Selected Writings* (The Hague: Mouton, 1981), esp. 3:39, 99, 775.

15. Steven J. Mithen, *The Singing Neanderthal: The Origins of Music, Language, Mind, and Body* (Cambridge, Mass.: Harvard University Press, 2008).

16. Henri Meschonnic, *Critique du rythme* (Lagrasse: Verdier, 1982), 225; my translation from the French.

17. Ibid., 217.

18. Stephen Ramsay, *Reading Machines: Toward an Algorithmic Criticism* (Champaign: University of Illinois Press: 2011), 16.

19. As does Martin Gore in the song "Fly on the Windscreen," in Depeche Mode, *Black Celebration* (Mute Records, 1986).

20. TV on the Radio, "Repetition," in *Nine Types of Light* (Interscope, 2011).

21. Jacques Derrida, "What Is a 'Relevant' Translation?" *Critical Inquiry* 27, no. 2 (2001): 178.

22. David C. Rubin, *Memory in Oral Traditions* (New York: Oxford University Press, 1995), 192.

23. Northrop Frye, *Anatomy of Criticism* (Princeton, N.J.: Princeton University Press, 1957), 118–119.

24. See Ernst Mach's brief remark about "the novelist" and *Gedankenexperiment* in *Erkenntnis und Irrtum: Skizzen zur Psychologie der Forschung* (Leipzig: Barth, 1905), 183.

INDEX

IDIOM INVENTING WRITING THEORY

Jacques Lezra and Paul North, series editors

Werner Hamacher, *Minima Philologica*. Translated by Catharine Diehl and Jason Groves

Michal Ben-Naftali, *Chronicle of Separation: On Deconstruction's Disillusioned Love*. Translated by Mirjam Hadar. Foreword by Avital Ronell

Daniel Hoffman-Schwartz, Barbara Natalie Nagel, and Lauren Shizuko Stone, eds., *Flirtations: Rhetoric and Aesthetics This Side of Seduction*

Jean-Luc Nancy, *Intoxication*. Translated by Philip Armstrong

Márton Dornbach, *Receptive Spirit: German Idealism and the Dynamics of Cultural Transmission*

Sean Alexander Gurd, *Dissonance: Auditory Aesthetics in Ancient Greece*

Anthony Curtis Adler, *Celebricities: Media Culture and the Phenomenology of Gadget Commodity Life*

Nathan Brown, *The Limits of Fabrication: Materials Science, Materialist Poetics*

Jay Bernstein, Adi Ophir, and Ann Laura Stoler, eds., *Political Concepts: A Critical Lexicon*

Laurent Dubreuil, *Poetry and Mind: Tractatus Poetico-Philosophicus*